# The Essence of
# Successful
# Staff Selection

**The Essence of Management Series**

# The Essence of Successful Staff Selection

Ron Ludlow
Fergus Panton

**Prentice Hall**

New York   London   Toronto   Sydney   Tokyo   Singapore

First published 1991 by
Prentice Hall International (UK) Ltd
66 Wood Lane End, Hemel Hempstead
Hertfordshire HP2 4RG
A division of
Simon & Schuster International Group

Typeset in 10/12pt Palatino by
Keyset Composition, Colchester

Printed and bound in Great Britain by
BPCC Wheatons Ltd, Exeter

---

Library of Congress Cataloging-in-Publication Data

Ludlow, Ron.
    The essence of successful staff selection/Ron Ludlow, Fergus
Panton.
      p.  cm. — (The Essentials of management series)
      Includes bibliographical references and index.
      ISBN 0-13-284704-3
      1. Employee selection.   I. Panton, Fergus.   II. Title.
III. Series: Prentice Hall essentials of management series.
HF5549.5.S38L83   1991
658.3'112 – – dc20

90-7940
CIP

---

British Library Cataloguing in Publication Data

Ludlow, Ron
The essence of successful staff selection.
1. Personnel. Selection
I. Title  II. Panton, Fergus 1921–  III. Series
658.3112

ISBN 0-13-284704-3

1 2 3 4 5   95 94 93 92 91

# Contents

v

# 1

# The overall process

It has been found helpful, when introducing the topic of selection, to start with a brief summary of the total process. This enables one to see the elements that comprise it and how they interrelate.

An example of such a summary dealing with recruitment from outside the organization is given in Figure 1.1. The six boxes illustrate a step-by-step approach and indicate the need for analysis and planning in working out requirements, as an essential preliminary to obtaining applicants from whom a suitable person may be selected. The last two boxes provide a reminder that the process is not complete until the applicant has actually joined and that success or failure of the selection procedures can in the end only be judged by how well the individuals perform on the job.

Many managers, however, are more concerned with selection from within the organization and how to make good decisions about promotions and transfers, and the deployment and development of staff. In essence, they are interested in identifying potential and creating opportunities for it to be allowed to grow and expand. But they also know that the organization's needs must be met and its objectives achieved, and that there is likely to be conflict between these needs and the needs of the individual.

Figure 1.2 was designed with the intent of demonstrating how both kinds of selection might be combined in one model.

It is often argued that selection from outside the organization is more

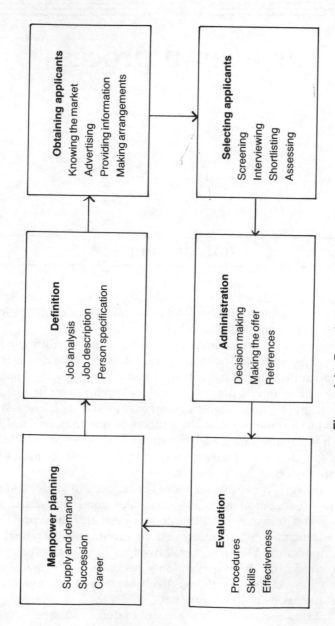

**Figure 1.1** Recruitment and selection

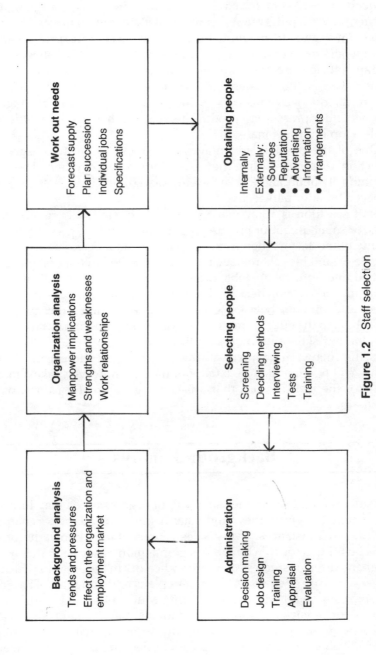

**Figure 1.2** Staff selection

difficult than selection from within. It is true, in theory at least, that the former requires judgements on much sketchier evidence and on very short timescales. In practice, however, especially in large organizations where the recruitment function is centralized, specialized expertise and efficient methods can ensure that a high performance standard is achieved. Unfortunately, it is not so easy within the working environment to establish the same controls; the busy manager is always under pressure to produce results and has had very little time to develop interpersonal skills.

One of the possible advantages of looking at the two aspects of selection together is that they complement each other. There are common elements and where the emphasis differs it can help give each aspect a broader perspective.

Staff selection is a key managerial activity since all organizations, large or small, public or private, depend on people to produce results. Many other factors determine organizational performance, but if people of suitable calibre have not been recruited in the first place and slotted into appropriate jobs, organizational objectives will suffer. So every time a selection decision has to be made we must ensure that we have, and pursue, policies, practices, systems and procedures that contribute to the effectiveness of that decision, and that we continue to develop our skills and understanding.

In the following chapters all the elements mentioned in the two charts will be examined in detail. Let us first, however, take a look at some of the broad issues that arise, using Figure 1.2 as a basis for discussion.

## Background analysis

The success, and sometimes survival, of organizations may hinge on the extent to which they understand and can adapt to changing external circumstances. Every sales representative knows he or she must be fully in touch with what is going on in his or her patch. Every company director studies economic indicators in the areas in which his or her company operates. All business plans and budgets are based on assumptions about the environment. Much time and effort is expended on analysis, as every student of management appreciates when he or she grapples with the mysteries of that elusive subject called 'business policy'. Trends are identified and analyzed, as well as their probable effect on the financial viability of the organization. If, for

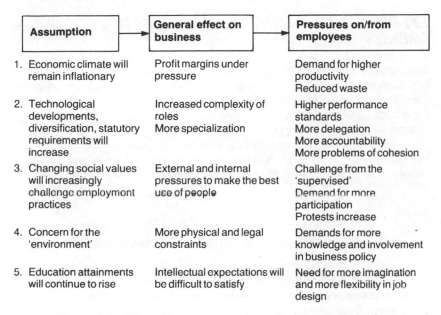

| Assumption | General effect on business | Pressures on/from employees |
|---|---|---|
| 1. Economic climate will remain inflationary | Profit margins under pressure | Demand for higher productivity<br>Reduced waste |
| 2. Technological developments, diversification, statutory requirements will increase | Increased complexity of roles<br>More specialization | Higher performance standards<br>More delegation<br>More accountability<br>More problems of cohesion |
| 3. Changing social values will increasingly challenge employment practices | External and internal pressures to make the best use of people | Challenge from the 'supervised'<br>Demand for more participation<br>Protests increase |
| 4. Concern for the 'environment' | More physical and legal constraints | Demands for more knowledge and involvement in business policy |
| 5. Education attainments will continue to rise | Intellectual expectations will be difficult to satisfy | Need for more imagination and more flexibility in job design |

**Figure 1.3**  Effect of social, technological and political trends

example, it is assumed that the economic climate will remain inflationary, top management will see their profit margins threatened. This has implications for the internal working of the organization: they tend to put pressure on middle management to 'tighten their belts' and this in turn leads to pressure on employees in the shape of demands for higher productivity and a reduction of waste.

Figure 1.3 gives further examples of how social, technological and political trends may affect the business and, in turn, individual employers, groups of employees and the employment market as a whole. This particular set of assumptions was reached after discussions about how to increase employee imvolvement in the management of a business. The discussions had intrinsic value in that they improved mutual understanding. They were probably more significant than the conclusions reached. As a method of analysis, it can be recommended. You are therefore invited either individually or in groups to undergo the following exercise.

## EXERCISE 1.1   ANALYZING EMPLOYEE RELATIONS TRENDS

Every organization is affected by the environment in which it operates and also exerts influence on it. Each employee is the product of the community in which he lives. Socioeconomic and political pressures have direct impact on both the organization and the employees, creating needs which may lead them to act in divergent ways and be in conflict.

As employee relations is an area where the pace of change is becoming increasingly rapid, it is important to keep abreast of external trends and pressures so that the key issues needing attention can be defined in time.

### Task

You are asked to discuss each statement that appears below, and determine the following:

1.   What general effect it will have on the organization.
2.   What pressures it will create on employees as a whole and on any particular group of employees.

### Economic factors

- Economic growth will be variable and minimal.
- Government will increasingly intervene in industry.
- The economic climate will remain inflationary.
- Industry will continue to favour labour reducing investment.
- Unemployment will continue at a high level.

### Social factors

- Companies will be increasingly required to show concern about pollution and conservation issues.
- People will place less value on work or career as a total life concern. Jobs will increasingly be regarded as a means to an end.
- As educational attainments rise in both depth of knowledge and in total number, intellectual expectations will be difficult to satisfy.
- Loyalty to the organization will be replaced by loyalty to professions and skilled trades.

## Organizational

- Decreasing influence of traditional power structures on employees at all levels, e.g. shareholders, unions.
- Increased professionalization of management.
- Need to develop interface skills will increase.
- An increase in both the quality and the quantity of information to be managed, which in turn will lead to changes in the distribution of power.

## Technological

- The rate and impact of technological invention will continue to rise and lead to increased complexity in managerial roles.
- Technological applications will be increasingly inhibited by social/environmental factors.
- More consultation with those concerned prior to making a heavy investment in high technology.
- Need for a more flexible approach to return on investment.

Similar questions of more immediate concern to particular organizations could readily be added. But if you decide to hold group discussions, plenty of time should be allocated!

---

# Organization analysis

---

Having established its short-, medium- and long-term objectives, the organization has to identify and assess its immediate and future manpower requirements in both quantitative and qualitative terms. This is part of the process – often called the 'demand' side – of manpower planning. It entails: (a) breaking down organization objectives (what are we aiming to do) into plans (how and when are we going to achieve them); (b) assessing the extent to which current resources are adequate or could be made so by redeployment; and (c) determining the shortfall and therefore identifying recruitment needs. Stated like this, the task seems straightforward enough, but there are many complications. As organizations grow in size and sophistication they need to change their manpower. The skills and abilities that were suitable in the past may no longer be applicable and present staff may not be able to perform future jobs. Further, human resources take time to develop and even if current employees have the capacity to learn, the rate and impact of changing objectives may not make training a feasible option.

As noted above, individual needs may well differ from the organization's perceived needs. Ideally both sets of needs should be taken into account and some sort of compromise achieved. If they are not, the individual may leave or, perhaps worse, become a minimal performer. It pays to bear in mind that all employees need to know: (a) what the future holds for them; (b) that the organization recognizes their talents and will strive to use them: and (c) that their aspirations will be taken into account when their work and careers are being planned.

Regular reviews of the organization's operations should be made in order to determine the strengths and weaknesses of its structure, the design of its jobs and the nature of the working relationships between and within groups. It is a common research finding that talent is underutilized, and that we should perhaps look carefully at the staff we have before embarking on a recruitment programme. Equally, it is important to look for gaps in the total knowledge and skills of the staff and guard against possible obsolescence.

## Working out needs

What the organization assesses it requires – the 'supply' side of manpower planning – may not be realizable, for shortages of skilled staff can still occur even in areas of high unemployment. Sometimes, however, these shortages are the result of failure to look sufficiently far ahead at the recruiting stage, of failure to make succession plans to cover predictable changes through retirement, promotion or wastage.

The key to successful planning lies in analyzing the demands of the jobs for which replacements will be required and then establishing which subordinate jobs contain critical elements of the target jobs so that relevant experience can be obtained. This is the concept of 'feeder' jobs of which there are likely to be several to each target job. They may be identified in different functions/departments/sections.

We cannot therefore work out requirements without a thorough analysis of jobs. We need to know what tasks have to be performed, what problems have to be handled, what knowledge, experience and skills are needed, and what personal qualities are desirable. The end result of job analysis is a job description which contains the information that enables you to specify the kind of person best suited to fill the job. Selection from outside cannot be done efficiently without such a specification, and selection from within could be greatly improved if the same technique were applied.

# Obtaining people

## From inside

In order to make successful staff selections from within the organization, it is essential that up-to-date information is available on what work people have done and how well it has been performed. Such records should be consistent, accurate, comprehensive and objective. The main source of this information will be the appraisal system.

The way the system is designed and applied will clearly play a significant part in the identification of potential. To obtain optimum results, it should possess the following features:

1. It should complement the process of work planning and review used in day-to-day management by providing an opportunity for longer-term, more comprehensive review sessions.
2. The appraisal meeting should be conducted on joint problem-solving lines. Boss and subordinate jointly reach agreement about their work, where they are going, how they are doing and what action can be taken to improve their related performance.
3. The appraisal process should provide those being appraised with an opportunity to talk about their performance, development plans and future career.
4. The outcome of the discussions should be recorded so that senior management can obtain feedback on current performance, and estimate potential and individual aspirations which will help them to see who is able to contribute what to the future of the organization and to make appropriate decisions.

Career planning, essentially an individual matter, is part of the appraisal process as well as an activity that follows on from it. By setting out to create opportunities for individual development, it enables people both to learn from experience and to show their potential.

The appraisal process is the key factor in identifying potential in the total management system, but it has to be fully integrated with the work-planning and man-management systems. It cannot function effectively in isolation from manpower planning and all the related activities.

Large organizations employ staff to provide a training and development service. In small concerns the responsibility for the function becomes one of many that each manager has to assume. Attitudes vary enormously: some consider the training and development of their subordinates as a prime responsibility; others consider it a millstone round their necks, a hindrance to 'getting on with the job'. There can be little doubt, however, that training and development activities can assist the process of selecting from within, not just in providing knowledge and developing skills but also in helping individuals and the organization to identify potential. There is, again, an inherent risk of a conflict of values between the organization's view of its needs and individual needs. Training sessions, whether formal or on the job, are frequently used – some would say abused – as vehicles for assessment. Questions such as 'Is the content and method used relevant to present or future jobs?', 'What relationship is there between course performance and performance on the job?', 'How competent and objective are the observers?', and 'Do the participants know they are being assessed?' raise ethical issues and create controversy.

Two points seem worth emphasizing. First, there are so many variables in the job situation, especially at managerial levels, that few jobs have identical requirements. There are differences in working environments and the nature and intensity of problems that have to be solved. No standard blend of characteristics and abilities will meet all requirements and the 'syllabus' approach to training is misguided. Second, people undergoing training and development activities must know whether they are being assessed and what use is being made of assessments; otherwise confidence and trust will be destroyed. If they are being assessed, there must be discussion sessions built into the programme so that they have an opportunity to express their views and where appropriate challenge the validity of the assessments.

Perhaps the most valuable contribution that those involved in the training and development function can make is in helping to analyze and clarify the problems. The process that they have to pursue in the normal course of their work has much in common with the process of identifying potential. Indeed it can be argued that judgements about a person's suitability for promotion are greatly influenced by his drive to learn and capacity for learning, i.e. his 'trainability'. These are qualities which every training man is quick to perceive, and he sees them in relation, broadly speaking, to defined needs in knowledge and skills.

For example, for managers, the starting-point for determining the training approach is as follows:

1. Knowledge:   What knowledge is required now and in the future of his own function, other functions, the industry, general management, and external trends and pressures.
2. Skills:   What is required now and in the future as regards functional (e.g. financial, research, technical), problem-solving (e.g. everything concerned with the use of intelligence), and human (e.g. everything concerned with personal relationships) skills.

## From outside

Enough has been said about the issues involved in successful staff selection from within to indicate that it is no easy matter. People do not have to be 'obtained' in the recruitment sense: they are already there. But their presence may not be evident; their virtues may be obscured. It is in the 'obtaining people' element of the process that the greatest divergence occurs between the two forms of selection, for a great deal of work has to be done to attract a large field of good candidates and conversely discourage unsuitable ones from applying. It is a crucial part of the process. At this juncture, it may be sufficient to say that, having formed a mental picture of the ideal candidate, through job analysis and person specification, we have to decide how we are going to reach our target audience. Time spent on establishing contacts with potential sources of candidates is seldom wasted, but when a vacancy has to be filled the alternative methods open to us have to be compared in terms of cost and the time available. If the reputation of the organization is that it is a 'good employer', this can be a great help. Likewise, well-produced public relations material makes the task easier. Advertising, although important, is only one means of assembling the people we want in order to make a good selection.

# Selecting people

We have already touched on some aspects of assessing people and emphasis was placed on assessments being work-related. Selecting people from outside creates greater demands because of severe time constraints; but fundamentally the issues are the same. Selection necessitates two complex activities: (a) assessing ability and personality, and (b) predicting how individuals will behave in the future.

This is the fascination and challenge. We all have our own ideas about what qualities are important. We may have been fortunate enough to have worked under someone who inspired us, and terms such as leadership, initiative and perception spring easily to our lips. The trouble is, however, that words like leadership, initiative, etc., are abstract, difficult to define and almost impossible to measure. Using checklists for assessment purposes, where the assessor is asked to mark on a five- or seven-point scale how much 'initiative' an individual has, is clearly nonsensical and worthless. Yet such systems are still commonly used and it is hardly surprising if faulty selection decisions ensue.

Essentially the assessment of an external candidate must be made on the information recorded on his application form or CV, on impressions gained during interviews and/or through psychological/aptitude tests or group selection methods (often called assessment centres). How we go about achieving this will emerge later.

# Administration

All recruiters and selectors need to remind themselves occasionally that selection is a two-way process. It is one thing to make a decision about which of the applicants you want; it is quite another matter to get them to join, and to ensure that they remain motivated in their work in the critical first few months after appointment. Indeed if there is a high turnover in this period, it will be obvious that something was wrong with the selection process, the initial induction training or the job design.

In this stage of the proceedings, a high degree of administrative efficiency is called for. The conditions of work, the remuneration level and benefits have to be spelt out, references taken up and initial training organized.

By way of summarizing what the selection process is trying to achieve, it may be appropriate to offer a definition of purpose which is as follows: 'To ensure that suitable people are obtained to meet the organization's immediate and longer-term requirements, while at the same time taking into account the individuals' needs and aspirations.'

To conclude this introductory chapter we have included in Exercise

*Faulties once joined?*
*PC Joined*
*Training*

1.2 five short case studies which are representative of the issues encountered in selection work. If they are used for group discussion purposes it is suggested that small groups of four to five are given no more than forty minutes to produce verbal reports for more general discussion.

## EXERCISE 1.2

### Political pressures:   Case 1

You are the general manager of a subsidiary of a large international company operating in the Indian subcontinent. Your company's prosperity and survival are strongly affected by your standing with government and by the way you take into account political issues when making your business decisions. Your parent company has stressed the importance of maintaining good public relations.

The political scene is fairly quiet at the moment, although there are increasing reports of student unrest and militant threats from unemployed graduates. These rumblings have led government to put considerable pressure on industry to take on more graduates.

It so happens that your work has expanded partly due to government contracts, and you need to take on some twenty-five additional office staff to cope with the administrative load. As the quality of work of your current clerical staff is rather poor, you are tempted to fill most of the twenty-five vacancies from the unemployed graduates. This would ensure a higher level of ability and at the same time stand you in good stead with government.

Some of your managers think you should resist government pressure as a matter of principle. Others are not very keen on having too many graduates around, although their reasons are not very clear and they may simply be prejudiced.

What would you do?

### Training and selection:   Case 2

You and your colleagues are worried about the quality of your first-line supervision. You feel that the low standard may be due to faults in the way they were selected in the past, but you are very aware that they were given little help or training when first promoted. The supervisors say they were 'thrown in at the deep end', but they have no great faith in formal training and are adamant that the company should continue their policy of promotion from within.

You know that a company in the same line of business has been running two-day courses for potential supervisors for some time – apparently with success. You have been given an opportunity to visit them, and although you have doubts about the scheme you decide to go.

What would you try to find out?

## Shortage of skilled staff:    Case 3

You are a partner in a small high-technology company that could expand rapidly if you could obtain the staff you require; but there is a national shortage of skilled staff at technician, analyst and managerial levels.

You consider that you need either to take on a part-time personnel officer or to seek help from a recruitment consultant, but you do not much like the idea of having to poach staff from companies in your line of business and you have heard stories about head-hunters being cowboys and charging heavy fees.

What steps would you take to get the kind of help you require?

## Selection policy:    Case 4

You are successfully running a company somewhere in the Middle East and have been depending largely on expatriate staff to get your results. Government, however, has started to put restrictions on entry permits and visas because it understandably wishes to encourage local recruitment. You accept the logic of their thinking and were in any case contemplating replacing expatriates with local nationals at managerial level because of their knowledge of the country and because you could reduce staff overheads considerably.

One of the potential difficulties in doing this was brought home to you when a very senior official rang you up and said that he had heard of your plans and that he had just the right man for you. He knew him well, as he was his nephew.

You wonder what policy to adopt so that what you do can be seen to be fair.

## Career prospects:    Case 5

Research shows that what most people are looking for when they move jobs are better career prospects, more freedom to make decisions and more use being made of their talents. Yet much of conventional recruitment concentrates on the job to be done rather than the job opportunities in the organization in the future.

You have recently been appointed managing director (MD) of a medium-sized company with a specific brief to bring about expansion through change. You find that in the past people have been taken on for posts rather than to work for the company. You want a more flexible approach to recruitment and selection.

How are you going to effect a change?

# 2

# Organizational analysis

Management is concerned with turning resources into results; managing people is a part of the process and an important part. So that we make the best decisions about selection from within and recruitment from outside, we need to take stock of the way we manage people in our organization and how effective we are.

We hear much nowadays about the importance of productivity. Newspapers publish league tables that show how different nations compare in economic performance. The money market employs a host of analysts whose sole job is to study how companies are doing and make predictions about their future results.

To some, productivity is essentially a matter of financial ratios. Clearly, genuine improvements in productivity can be achieved by increasing investment and through technical innovation, increased mechanization and product rationalization, but critical to the long-term success of these operations is the way the human effort is managed and the way people can be he'ped to adapt to the changes that are inevitably involved.

An analysis of the situations where **high productivity** from people is achieved indicates that many of the following characteristics are likely to apply:

1.  Both individually and in groups, employees have the opportunity to work on tasks which they understand and which contribute to the organization's objectives.
2.  They are suited to the work, they can get on with the job with the right tools, skills and information, and problems are resolved quickly and satisfactorily.

3. They are able to work together effectively in groups, where appropriate, and with other groups, and when disagreements occur they are resolved satisfactorily; there is an atmosphere of trust.

4. They are able to contribute their effort, ideas and creativity and therefore have the opportunity to develop.

5. They have the will to work; they understand, support and take responsibility for achieving the results required.

Conversely, the characteristics of **low productivity** situations indicate the following:

1. Changes are introduced without participation or explanation.
2. Tasks are unclear.
3. Tasks are not clearly related to the organization's objectives.
4. Jobs are boring, monotonous and uninteresting; there is no scope for contributing.
5. The workplace is badly designed.
6. Knowledge, skill and talents that are available are not used in the task.
7. People are in the wrong place for their talents.
8. Responsibility is obscure or located too far from the work to which it relates.
9. Information is inappropriate, inadequate, late or not available to the right person.
10. Achievements are not identified for the individual, for groups or for the organization.
11. Management methods and style are inappropriate for those being managed.
12. Managers change frequently and their style is inconsistent.
13. People feel their reward is unfair.
14. People feel they cannot influence constructively the events in the organization that concern them.
15. People feel insecure.

To improve productivity, therefore, we need to capture and retain the beneficial elements of the high productivity factors.

These two sets of characteristics were once shown to a senior manager in one of the leading UK motor manufacturing companies. They were shown rather tentatively, as it was felt that the point may have been overlaboured. He studied the paper in silence and then said 'By God, what has been written here about low productivity characteristics is the best summary of my company and what is wrong with it that I have ever seen!'

Be that as it may, it is suggested that organizations will improve productivity if they concentrate their efforts on the following:

1.  Clarifying information about jobs and the characteristics and skills that are needed for effective performance.

2.  Finding the right people initially and for subsequent transfer and promotion by using and developing techniques for selection and identification of potential.

3.  Designing jobs and structuring the organization in ways which will provide satisfaction.

4.  Understanding the need to work participatively with individuals and groups in planning the work, establishing productivity measurements and standards, solving the problems, delegating appropriate responsibility and judging the achievements.

5.  Ensuring that appropriate information is available at the right time in understandable form.

6.  Providing development opportunities for their staff.

7.  Monitoring external trends and pressures that are likely to affect the behaviour of people at work, planning for them and forecasting the changing demands likely to be made.

Here we may have the beginnings of a blueprint, but in no way does it tell us how we might get to where we want to go. Very large organizations employ or hire experts to devise means of providing the information to help them develop solutions. The behavioural and statistical techniques used are often highly complex. Most of us, however, do not have access to such facilities, nor may the funds be available.

Three tried and tested ways of analyzing the organization which do not require any specialized knowledge to administer are given here. The first instrument is a form of structured communications (Exercise 2.1). The array comprises sixteen statements. Participants are asked to select the three statements from the total which in their view most represent priority areas for attention. Each participant does this individually. The choices are recorded in public so that everyone can see how what they have selected relates to the general view. It can provide a powerful stimulus for discussion as well as an economic means of reaching consensus.

## EXERCISE 2.1   WE COULD IMPROVE IF:

| | | | |
|---|---|---|---|
| 1. More effort were made to match individuals' needs with those of the organization | 2. Operational plans were not made without prior consideration of manpower implications | 3. We ensured that the supply of manpower more closely met demand | 4. The impact of socioeconomic trends and pressures on all employees were systematically assessed |
| 5. Succession and career plans were more effectively formulated, reviewed and communicated | 6. Statistical data on turnover, manning, absenteeism, etc., were more readily available | 7. More effective use were made of individual talent and potential | 8. Employees were involved in setting targets and reviewing results of their work |
| 9. The process of sharing information about the organization's plans were systematically implemented | 10. Job responsibilities were more effectively analyzed and evaluated | 11. Appraisals were strictly related to work performance and substantiated by fact | 12. Recruitment and selection processes produced a higher quality standard on entry |
| 13. Training policies and objectives were designed to help people overcome problems in the work situation | 14. People were recompensed for achievement and merit | 15. Pay systems were consistently and universally applied | 16. Managers understood their organization's policies towards trade unions and their own role in IR |

## EXERCISE 2.2

A further, perhaps more familiar technique uses the idea of paired comparisons. Eight items have been selected. Participants are asked to accept the definitions supplied for the purposes of the exercise and say of each pair which they consider the more important. If, for example, in the first comparison 'rewards' has the edge over 'work planning', they put an X in the rewards column. When all twenty-eight comparisons have been recorded, the number of Xs in each vertical column is added up and ranked in order by each individual. The group's results are totalled to provide a basis for discussion and if desirable a means of agreeing action plans.

Name ................................

## Improving managerial effectiveness

What do you consider to be the best ways to improve managerial effectiveness in your organization?

Eight possible approaches have been selected and are described on the attached sheet. Please study them. Then ask yourself each question in turn and put an X in the appropriate column on the right.

Do you attach more importance to improving:

| | INITIAL SELECTION | JOB DESIGN | REWARDS | WORK RELATIONSHIPS | WORK PLANNING | PERFORMANCE APPRAISAL | NEEDS ANALYSIS | TALENT UTILIZATION |
|---|---|---|---|---|---|---|---|---|
| 1. WORK PLANNING or REWARDS | | | | | | | | |
| 2. INITIAL SELECTION or NEEDS ANALYSIS | | | | | | | | |
| 3. JOB DESIGN or PERFORMANCE APPRAISAL | | | | | | | | |
| 4. TALENT UTILIZATION or WORK RELATIONSHIPS | | | | | | | | |
| 5. NEEDS ANALYSIS or WORK PLANNING | | | | | | | | |
| 6. PERFORMANCE APPRAISAL or INITIAL SELECTION | | | | | | | | |
| 7. WORK RELATIONSHIPS or JOB DESIGN | | | | | | | | |
| 8. REWARDS or TALENT UTILIZATION | | | | | | | | |

| | TALENT UTILIZATION | NEEDS ANALYSIS | PERFORMANCE APPRAISAL | WORK PLANNING | WORK RELATIONSHIPS | REWARDS | JOB DESIGN | INITIAL SELECTION |
|---|---|---|---|---|---|---|---|---|
| 9. WORK PLANNING or PERFORMANCE APPRAISAL | | | | | | | | |
| 10. INITIAL SELECTION or REWARDS | | | | | | | | |
| 11. NEEDS ANALYSIS or JOB DESIGN | | | | | | | | |
| 12. JOB DESIGN or INITIAL SELECTION | | | | | | | | |
| 13. REWARDS or WORK RELATIONSHIPS | | | | | | | | |
| 14. PERFORMANCE APPRAISAL or NEEDS ANALYSIS | | | | | | | | |
| 15. WORK PLANNING or WORK RELATIONSHIPS | | | | | | | | |
| 16. TALENT UTILIZATION or INITIAL SELECTION | | | | | | | | |
| 17. WORK RELATIONSHIPS or PERFORMANCE APPRAISAL | | | | | | | | |
| 18. NEEDS ANALYSIS or TALENT UTILIZATION | | | | | | | | |
| 19. INITIAL SELECTION or WORK PLANNING | | | | | | | | |

| | INITIAL SELECTION | JOB DESIGN | REWARDS | WORK RELATIONSHIPS | WORK PLANNING | PERFORMANCE APPRAISAL | NEEDS ANALYSIS | TALENT UTILIZATION |
|---|---|---|---|---|---|---|---|---|
| 20. JOB DESIGN or REWARDS | | | | | | | | |
| 21. PERFORMANCE APPRAISAL or TALENT UTILIZATION | | | | | | | | |
| 22. WORK PLANNING or JOB DESIGN | | | | | | | | |
| 23. REWARDS or NEEDS ANALYSIS | | | | | | | | |
| 24. TALENT UTILIZATION or WORK PLANNING | | | | | | | | |
| 25. WORK RELATIONSHIPS or INITIAL SELECTION | | | | | | | | |
| 26. REWARDS or PERFORMANCE APPRAISAL | | | | | | | | |
| 27. NEEDS ANALYSIS or WORK RELATIONSHIPS | | | | | | | | |
| 28. TALENT UTILIZATION or JOB DESIGN | | | | | | | | |
| SUM Add up the number of Xs | | | | | | | | |
| RANK | | | | | | | | |
| COMPARISON with | | | | | | | | |

*Approaches to improving managerial effectiveness*

INITIAL SELECTION:  Raising entry standards, improving methods and skills of selectors.

JOB DESIGN:  Clarifying accountabilities, increasing the degree of autonomy in decision making and generally considering motivational factors.

REWARDS:  Ensuring that the remuneration package (e.g. pay, allowances, pension, etc.) is attractive and that merit and effort are rewarded.

WORK RELATIONSHIPS:  Improving mutual understanding between jobholders, their bosses, colleagues and subordinates.

WORK PLANNING:  Establishing work priorities, agreeing performance standards and individual action plans.

PERFORMANCE APPRAISAL:  Discussing results achieved against agreed plans, assessing performance and recording the outcome.

NEEDS ANALYSIS:  Identifying individual training and development needs and ambitions, and reconciling them with organizational needs.

TALENT UTILIZATION:  Identifying underutilized talent and potential, and planning career and promotion paths.

As an alternative to these two exercises, or to complement them, Exercise 2.3 is self-explanatory.

## EXERCISE 2.3

## Auditing the way we manage people

We need to take stock periodically – perhaps regularly – of the company situation, to diagnose the problems, issues and opportunities, and to examine whether our personnel policies and practices need revision or updating.

To improve what we do and how we do it, it may be helpful to think in terms of the concepts which underlie our policies; the processes which translate these policies into practice, and the efficiency and skill with which we implement them; and the attitudes and feeling of people – how they react and interact.

### Task

As a preliminary step to devising action plans to suit the needs of your own organization, please discuss Checklist 2.1 and select the items which call for priority of attention in your group as a whole.

---

# CHECKLIST 2.1

---

# Manpower planning

1. When corporate objectives and plans are reviewed, is adequate time set aside to discuss the manpower implications in both the short and the long term?

2. Are external trends and influences – technological, social, political, economic and legislative – systematically and fully analyzed to assess their probable impact on staffing the organization?

3. Are up-to-date records, inventories and procedures maintained and regularly analyzed so that basic planning and control information is provided?

4. Is the quality of the information about people adequate? Is it consistent, comprehensive, accurate and fair?

5. Are succession plans covering immediate replacements (unexpected losses, sickness, attachments, etc.), predictable changes up to five years ahead (promotions, retirements, etc.) and other longer-term needs

24

(reorganization, retirement expansion) formulated and thoroughly reviewed annually?

## Recruitment and selection

6. Are adequate job descriptions and person specifications produced for all vacancies?
7. Are effective contacts maintained with all potential sources of staff and labour?
8. Do testing methods need updating and extending?
9. Could group selection methods be used?
10. Is the effectiveness of the selection process regularly reviewed and monitored?

## Planning and appraisal

11. Are work structures, roles, relationships, responsibilities and levels of authority continuously reviewed to assess their appropriateness in both task and development terms?
12. Is job content regularly reviewed with the jobholder to determine what scope there is for job redesign and to make more use of potential?
13. Is the appraisal meeting conducted on joint problem-solving lines? Do boss and subordinate work together to agree work targets and improve mutual understanding?
14. Does the appraisee have an opportunity to talk about his performance and future development?
15. Are assessments strictly related to work performance and substantiated by factual examples?

## Training and development

16. Are training policies and objectives designed to:
    (a) contribute to the organization's short- and long-term operating objectives?
    (b) support the fact that most training takes place on the job?
    (c) assist people to overcome problems they have in their work?
17. Does the training and development process help teams and groups to operate as effectively as individuals?

## Communications

18. Are face-to-face briefing procedures for explaining management decisions followed with conviction?

19. Are employees:
    (a) given information about developments before they take place?
    (b) given opportunities to put their point of view with the knowledge that it will be seriously considered?
    (c) involved in setting targets, in reviewing the results of their work and in all decisions that affect them?

20. Is the process of sharing information on the organization's plans systematically implemented and are opportunities to contribute to the formulation of plans encouraged?

21. Are working relationships within groups and between groups reviewed and evaluated by those groups?

## Remuneration

22. Are jobs analyzed and evaluated in a consistent and systematic fashion?

23. Do both managers and employees understand the general principles of the evaluation system?

24. Have salary planning guidelines been established?

---

All these instruments can be used on management courses to provoke discussion and increase awareness, but their greatest value is when they are used in the work situation and are related to actual as opposed to theoretical considerations.

Communication upward can be a major problem in most organizations large or small. It is best therefore that initial discussions are conducted in peer groups, as employees may be reluctant to appear critical of their seniors and unwilling to risk damage to their prospects. Top management really needs to set an example and if it is made of stern stuff, it will be prepared to accept that its view of itself is not necessarily shared by those below.

A survey conducted in a major retail organization was based on a structured communication approach similar to the one in Exercise 2.1. They were not satisfied with their performance appraisal system and were seeking to improve it. Top management agreed to subject themselves to the same process that they were proposing to ask all their managers to undergo. Four broad levels of management were involved. It was fascinating to observe how each level of management saw the others and how often their assumptions were wildly inaccurate. In fact the degree of consensus about the health of the organization and the remedial measures needed to improve it was quite remarkable. It meant that when the improvement programme was introduced, it stood a fair chance of acceptance in what is a notoriously sensitive area.

If it is apparent that there are relationship problems between groups (e.g. sales and production, accounts v. personnel), these instruments can be used to identify more clearly the nature of the problem and the degree of differences of opinion. They can thus help organizations to become more aware of the impact on job structures and job design of internal relationships. Problems need to be faced if organizations are to survive and grow.

We have been dealing of course with only those aspects of organization analysis which have a bearing on the subject matter of the book. The kinds of issues raised affect both forms of selection, and have particular relevance when internal and external selection is determined for development purposes rather than specific tasks that have to be performed.

What we have been trying to advocate is the avoidance of too mechanical and narrow an approach to staff selection. We strongly maintain that the acquisition and retention of good-quality staff will not be achieved as long as staffing and employment decisions are regarded as a management prerogative. Successful staff selection is much more likely to occur if a more reciprocal approach is followed.

To conclude this chapter, Figure 2.1 summarizes the influences operating on both organizations and individuals and how they interact. These interactions operate both inwardly and outwardly on the hierarchical structure from the lowest and most specific levels to the highest and most general levels shown by the concentric circles.

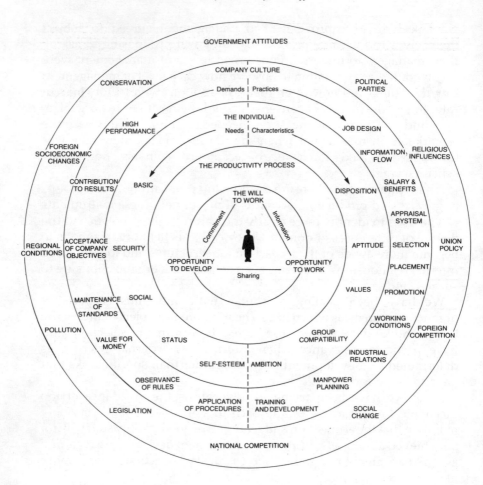

**Figure 2.1** Socioeconomic pressures

# 3

# Working out requirements

## Preamble

Figure 3.1 restates in diagrammatic form the essential factors involved in successful staff selection. It also illustrates the need for reconciling the different perspectives each contributes, and the way they interconnect and interrelate.

In large firms and organizations, the analysis and planning of requirements have been greatly facilitated by computer-based management information systems designed to meet their specific needs. Many of the important decisions, however, are of a qualitative nature, involve the use of judgement and cannot be resolved by mathematical or statistical techniques. Excessive number-crunching has to be resisted!

For the many managers who work in small units, staff selection is almost exclusively an individual matter. Even in the mammoth organization, the point comes when the critical decision is whether or not to promote person A to job X; or when to recruit someone for job Y.

## The analysis and description of managerial work

In the cold light of day, the advantages to everyone of accurately describing what work an individual has to undertake in return for the

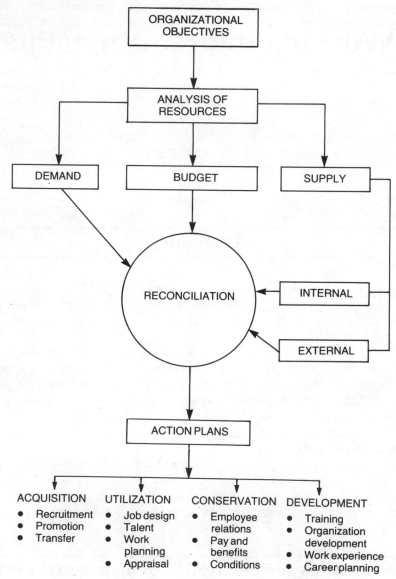

**Figure 3.1**  Human resource management

pay received are so obvious that no explanation should be necessary. The wide range of opinions, often extreme, that traditional ways of describing jobs provoke does however suggest that the topic needs approaching with an element of caution. Attitudes can be highly emotional. For some, a job description conjures up visions of boring statements of duties to be performed. It smacks of an unimaginative control device designed to chain employees to their desks or benches. Other managers, sometimes with justification, see job descriptions as a kind of strait-jacket that prevents them from allocating work to their employees that operational circumstances demand.

Probably, however, what has created managerial opposition to job descriptions is not so much the uses to which they are put but the inadequacy of what is written. The precursor to a job description is the activity called job analysis – the study of the work a person does.

It is a much more difficult process than it first appears to be, for most jobs have imprecise elements and ambiguous relationships. It involves intellectual challenge because it deals with consideration of abstract concepts, such as delegation and authority, and their application in practice.

Moreover, jobs are dynamic. They are influenced by the nature of the person doing them – his temperament, intelligence, drive and enthusiasm – and the importance of fitting jobs to the individual rather than the other way round is becoming increasingly recognized as a critical motivational factor. Jobs are also dramatically influenced by the rapidly changing socioeconomic environment in which we work and the need for organizations to adapt their objectives in order to survive.

Although the purpose for which job analysis is being used will influence the nature of information sought and the format of the job description, the differences are more of emphasis and detail and are not fundamental. Whether we are concerned with selection, training or rewarding, we need to know the demands a job makes, the tasks that comprise it and the range and complexity of problems that the job has to handle. Here we will be primarily concerned with job analysis in relation to managerial and supervisory jobs, but the principles outlined can be applied to work at any level in the organization.

## Main uses of job analysis

**Recruitment and selection**  To provide information about the purpose, duties, responsibilities and relationships of the job and the physical, social and economic factors that affect it. From this information, it is possible to specify the characteristics of the person best fitted to do the job effectively.

**Training and development**  To supply a detailed breakdown of the various elements or tasks that comprise a job in order to define the knowledge, skills and attitudes that lead to effective performance in both current and future jobs.

**Remuneration**  To supply information to show the relative importance, complexity and magnitude of a range of jobs so that financial rewards may be geared as closely as possible to match the contribution and effort of individual employees and to establish relative values between different types of work.

**Organization development**  To re-examine the structure or content of jobs, and especially the relationship between jobs in order to ensure that the organization is flexible and can adapt to changing circumstances.

## What is managerial work?

Figure 3.2 offers summarized versions of the views of a number of eminent writers. Stated so boldly, they do not do justice to their work, but the list does show the range and variety of conclusions. The differences to some extent reflect changing social values. Also as a result of the contribution of the social scientists we understand much more about the realities of organizational behaviour than we did.

## The analysis of managerial work

In our own selection of headings which we use to describe managerial work, we recognize our dependence upon the method of analysis invented by the management consultants Hay/MSL Limited. This was initially introduced for managerial job evaluation purposes and has been widely adopted in the public and private sectors. Its usefulness, however, extends much more widely than for remuneration purposes.

The following five headings ensure a reasonably comprehensive approach:

| FAYOL | <ul><li>analyzed operations into six main groups: technical, commercial, financial, security, accounting and administrative</li><li>broke down administration into five aspects: planning, organizing, commanding, coordinating and controlling</li></ul> |
|---|---|
| BARNARD | <ul><li>classified the functions of executives as<ul><li>providing the system of communication</li><li>promoting the security of essential efforts</li><li>formulating and defining purpose</li></ul></li></ul> |
| DRUCKER | <ul><li>quoted five basic operations:<ul><li>setting objectives</li><li>organizing work</li><li>motivating people and communicating with them</li><li>establishing measurable yardsticks</li><li>developing people</li></ul></li></ul> |
| JACQUES | <ul><li>defined management as 'the exercise of discretion within prescribed limits to attain goals/objectives'</li></ul> |
| BRECH | <ul><li>suggested six headings for job descriptions as having universal application:<ul><li>responsibility for</li><li>special responsibilities</li><li>limitations</li><li>subordinates</li><li>functional contacts</li><li>committees</li></ul></li></ul> |
| MINTZBERG | <ul><li>described managerial work in terms of roles<ul><li>interpersonal: figurehead, leader, liaison</li><li>informational: monitor, disseminator, spokesman</li><li>decision: entrepreneur, disturbance handler, resource allocator, negotiator</li></ul></li></ul> |

**Figure 3.2**  What is managerial work?

**Applying specialized knowledge, skills and experience**  We are concerned here with the *depth* of knowledge (technical, scientific, professional, managerial) and the *breadth* of knowledge (knowledge of the different elements, functions, the industry and the environment in order to plan and coordinate action).

**Making optimum use of physical and financial resources**  Here we look at the process of organizing, allocating and controlling the organization's resources. We need to assess the degree of accountability the individual has for money, stocks, plant, equipment, buildings and goodwill. Values need to be estimated.

**Effectively utilizing human resources**  This could be restated as 'the process of selecting, placing, motivating and developing people to meet their own and their organization's objectives'. Here one needs to take into account (a) the *numbers* of people directly and indirectly accountable to the jobholder, (b) the *level* and *qualifications*, and (c) *external* contacts.

**Making decisions and solving problems** Here we are concerned with the *nature* of the problems and decisions the jobholder handles – how frequently they recur, how important, how complex. We want to know what time and cost constraints he or she has to work within; the extent to which what he or she is allowed to do is governed by rules, procedures and policies; and the degree of uncertainty arising from lack of precedent.

**Using intelligence and imagination to create new ideas, techniques or systems** Here we are concerned with the intellectual challenge of the job, i.e. the nature of mental processes and the degree of freedom allowed to the individual to depart from accepted practices; or the degree of variation that is practicable.

## Who should write the description?

Most managers should be able to do this, given some guidelines and training. Skills in interviewing and writing come with experience. Qualities such as integrity and objectivity are clearly important. Credibility may more easily arise if an outside consultant is used but in many circumstances organizations must make the utmost use of their own resources. In large organizations, personnel departments may be able to supply the expertise or train and draw upon a team of analysts from all the functions.

Sources of information include present incumbents, immediate superiors, sometimes subordinates, observation of the job, training programmes and work plans/budgets. The main source of information about a job will in most cases be the person doing it. The analyst's task is to obtain a clear picture of the job that is being done, *what* there is to do, *how* it is done and *why* the job exists.

Many people are sensitive about their jobs and uncertain about how much trust they can afford to give – unfortunately, on occasion, with good reason. The job analyst may therefore be viewed with suspicion and there may be attempts to 'cover up' or mislead. It is therefore vital that the cooperation of the jobholder is sought and confidence maintained.

# How to approach the task

The approach can be divided into four parts:

1. Setting up the interview.
2. Conducting the interview.
3. Writing up the information.
4. Obtaining agreement.

1. Setting up the interview:

*explain what the job is and briefly give paper*

- Check that the jobholder has been briefed about the purpose of the interview and be prepared to explain your own approach.
- Fix a definite appointment with the jobholder, giving adequate notice.
- Allow at least two hours for the interview.
- Ensure that discussion can be private and free from interruptions.
- Ensure that the jobholder has easy access to any information/material he or she requires. Where possible, use his or her office.
- Study the checklist of questions and plan their use.

2. Conducting the interview:

- Go over the general background again and the reasons for the interview.
- Explain that he or she will have an opportunity to comment on what is written up about the job.
- Explain that the draft job description will be discussed at an interview with him or her and his/her boss.
- Start the interview with a subject that can be brought easily into the conversation. If there is no more appropriate starting-point ask the jobholder to sketch out an organization chart showing the jobs or functions reporting to him or her and also the other jobs reporting to his/her boss. This will usually indicate the line of questioning that should be followed.
- Let the interviewee do most of the talking, keeping the atmosphere informal and interjecting questions which direct the conversation into the areas to be explored.

- Search for facts and figures to substantiate the answers about the job. Remember that if the story does not seem to hang together properly, he or she is probably trying to make the job appear more important than it is.

- Get him or her to illustrate their statements with actual examples and record the most important ones.

- Do not spend too much time early on in trying to define 'purpose'. The real purpose will become more apparent after the accountabilities have been satisfactorily defined.

- Seek information that will enable judgements to be made about the nature and scope of the job in terms of the headings described under 'What is managerial work?' above.

- Refer to the questions in Checklist 3.1.

- Discuss a first draft of the accountabilities with the jobholder.

- As a way of opening up new areas to explore, ask the question 'What are the most important characteristics you would look for in a replacement?'

3.  Writing up the information:

- Having collected the information in a systematic way, it is important to present it in a systematic form that is easy and interesting to read. It should 'flow' naturally from one topic to the next, should pinpoint significant detail with clear examples ('for instance') but not 'bog down' the reader in trivialities.

- Above all it should try to convey a 'feel' for the job, its demands, its challenges, its frustrations, its excitements. 'Purpose' and 'Accountabilities', however, should be concise and precise.

- It is desirable in any one organization to have consistency in layout. The following headings are suggested:

  | | | |
  |---|---|---|
  | Name | Job title | Accountable to |
  | Department | Analyst | Date |
  | Purpose | | |
  | Dimensions | | |
  | Nature and scope | | |
  | Accountabilities | | |

4.  Obtaining agreement:

- It is good practice to prepare a first draft and clear it with the jobholder before going to the jobholder's boss.

- Be prepared and willing to negotiate two or three drafts as it is essential that both are completely happy with what has been written.
- It may be necessary to arrange a meeting between them and sometimes the analyst may have to approach a third party.

## CHECKLIST 3.1

The following checklist suggests the key issues that need to be raised in a job analysis interview. It is written in question form in the interests of brevity, but it will be seen that the questions overlap and are somewhat repetitive. They are not considered to be complete. The atmosphere created during the interview will largely determine which questions are most pertinent, how they should be phrased and in what sequence they are raised.

### What is the purpose of the job?

- What end results are to be accomplished by this job?
- What is the overall significance of the job from a company viewpoint?
- Why does this job exist?
- What is it paid for?

### What is the magnitude of the job?

- Find out the amount of money a year on which the job has impact. e.g. operating budget/sales volume/number of subordinates.
- Does the jobholder have a material effect on the amount of money spent by his or her department or the company? Is this effect reasonably consistent from year to year?
- Does he or she have a material effect that can be clearly defined on money *returned* to the company? Is it reasonably consistent from year to year?

### How does the job fit into the organization?

- For whom does he or she work directly?
- What other jobs report to the same boss?

- What are his or her most frequent contacts inside and outside the company?
- What committees does he or she serve on?
- Does he or she travel – where and why?

## What is the general composition of his or her supporting staff?

- What jobs report to him or her?
- Outline briefly the scope of each subordinate job – size, scope and reason for its existence.
- What sort of subordinates does he or she have – qualified, deeply experienced, etc.?
- How is control over subordinates' jobs exercised?
- What control information is used?
- With what subordinate position is there more direct contact?
- Does the jobholder need as much technical or specialist knowledge as the subordinate(s) and why?

## What is the general nature of technical, managerial and human relations know-how required?

- What are the basic challenges of the job?
- What is the technical/professional/economic environment in which the jobholder works?
- What specific fields of technical know-how are required – in order of importance? Follow through the sequence of events in the job: request actual examples of what he or she has been doing.
- How is the technical know-how acquired – academic training, experience on the job?
- What other sources of similar technical knowledge are there in the company – how much contact does he or she have with them?
- To what extent does the morale of his or her work group depend on him or her?
- Is he or she expected to run the team or to guide or coordinate its efforts?
- Does he or she have to persuade others – at own or senior level – to accept his or her ideas – in own or different fields?

- To what extent does the jobholder do the same sort of thing as the people who report to him or her?
- To whom does he or she go for help?
- To what extent is he or she free to 'go it alone'?
- What level of management looks to the jobholder for results, answers, service, etc.?
- What does he or she spend most time doing?
- In the day-to-day functioning of the job, how important is skill in dealing with human relations problems compared with technical knowledge?

## What are the key problems that must be solved by this job and how variable are they?

- What does the jobholder feel is the greatest challenge in the job?
- What are the most and least satisfying parts?
- What gives the jobholder greatest concern or worry in doing the work?
- Who or what guides his or her thinking on actions in these areas of concern?
- In what way does the boss provide guidance?
- How frequently does he or she go to the boss for help; or how frequently does the boss check/supervise the work?
- What type of problem does the jobholder deal with on his or her own authority?
- What type of problem does the jobholder refer to higher authority?
- How much does he or she rely on policy or precedent?
- Is each problem different and how?
- How predictable is the outcome?
- Are there guides or signposts to follow in solving the problems?
- Are the solutions available only by analyzing and interpreting what is known and building on that?
- Does he or she have any opportunity to tread completely new paths?
- Does he or she solve problems given to him/her or does he/she sense needs and recognize where work is needed?
- Does he or she analyze and clearly define the problems before starting work or is that done by the boss?

- Request examples of the problems that have arisen, how they have been solved and by whom.

## What is the nature and source of controls on his or her freedom to act or make decisions?

- What are the principal rules, regulations, precedents or personal control within which the jobholder operates?
- How frequently does he or she see the boss?
- What does he or she discuss with the boss?
- Can he or she change his/her own organization structure?
- Request examples of the most significant decisions or actions he or she takes.
- What authority has he or she on:
  - hiring and firing
  - capital expenditure
  - current expenditure
  - setting prices
  - changing methods
  - changing design, quality, policies or salaries?

## What important end results does the job exist to achieve?

- For what results, in addition to good problem-solving, is the jobholder held directly accountable?
- Is he or she fundamentally accountable for doing something or for seeing that it gets done by others?
- How are these results measured?
- Does he or she set objectives or organize to achieve objectives?
- Does he or she have a dominant impact over these results?

## Learning the analyst's job

Having had the privilege of initiating several hundred post-experience MBA students into the arts of job analysis, and having had to read an equal number of the job descriptions produced by them, we can state with some confidence where help is most commonly required.

As we all know, we all learn in different ways. It is hoped the preceding notes and guidelines have thrown a bit of light on the subject. But job analysis is an essentially practical activity and it can only really be learnt by doing it. People experienced in interviewing have little trouble in obtaining the information once they have grasped the purpose of the exercise. Time spent developing interviewing skills is therefore a necessity, as is time spent on writing up the job description. Exercise 3.1 concentrates exactly on these two needs.

### *EXERCISE 3.1    ANALYZE AND DESCRIBE*

Find a convivial soul who is prepared to be interviewed about his/her job and carry on as suggested. This is not so difficult as it sounds. Most people are interested in their jobs: some consider their work is not fully appreciated; some see an advantage in having a new description.

Students, of course, have no option but to pair up and do as they are told! It helps to reduce antipathy if their written work can earn them some recognition towards their results.

After this exercise is completed, it is very probable that a number of questions will arise which lead to further explanations and discussions. 'Purpose' and 'Accountability' always create problems, which is hardly surprising since experienced practitioners know how difficult it is to get them right. At this stage therefore it may be beneficial to issue some examples such as the ones that appear below.

## Examples

### Examples of purpose

1.  A general manager (of an overseas subsidiary): To maintain annual dividend pattern to shareholders, maximized within the limits acceptable to government, and at the same time secure the long-term viability of the company by providing consumer

satisfaction and by actively identifying the company with the growth and development of the country.

2. A sales manager:
   (a) To assist in achieving the company's marketing objectives by developing plans and strategy for his area of control.
   (b) By directing and controlling his or her field force staff, to achieve the agreed sales volume for his or her area working within an agreed budget.

3. A chief accountant:
   (a) To design and maintain up-to-date accounting policy guidelines and help the finance director develop financial policies.
   (b) To manage the accounting function in such a way as to:
   - ensure that assets are protected through control procedures and that statutory books of account are maintained
   - utilize to maximum advantage the company's currency resources and minimize foreign exchange exposure risks
   - provide financial advice and control information to managers and employees and foresee their future needs
   - produce the overall statutory company accounts.

4. A production director: To meet marketing department's delivery requirements of products continuously by overall planning and controlling of the production of the X factory; also meet export market requirements of raw materials from Y plant; and ensure that both plants maintain correct production standards at the most economical cost.

## Examples of accountabilities

1. A sales manager:
   (a) Developing the overall marketing plan and tactics for his or her area of control.
   (b) Assessing merchandising expenditure to accomplish marketing objectives.
   (c) Producing detailed plans for targeted volumes by accounts.
   (d) Implementing agreed plans through briefings and controls and assessing results by critique.
   (e) Ensuring staff is motivated and trained.
   (f) Controlling budget to plus or minus 5 per cent.

(g) Assessing what organization procedures and tehcniques are appropriate.

(h) Determining and controlling trade credits within laid-down limits.

2.  A chief accountant:

(a) Establishing accounting policy guidelines and procedures that will provide the internal service needed and also satisfy statutory/professional standards.

(b) Keeping the financial director informed about the financial state of the company.

(c) Training and developing accounting department staff to meet the demands of rapid expansion and a changing role.

(d) Ensuring that statutory books of account are correctly maintained.

(e) Protecting assets through control procedures and internal audits.

(f) Seeing that taxation returns are properly submitted.

(g) Ensuring that the company's currency resources are utilized to maximum advantage and that foreign exchange risks are minimized.

(h) Maximizing the advantages that can be obtained from computerization.

(i) Providing managers with the ongoing financial information they require to achieve results and foreseeing their future information needs.

(j) Keeping up to date on developments in accountancy theory and practice as well as in legislation.

One final point may be worth making about the implications of the choice of verbs used by the analyst in the description.

## WATCH YOUR VERBS

1.  **Policy making:** approve, authorize, define, determine, develop, direct, establish, plan.

2.  **Management:** achieve, assess, control, coordinate, ensure, identify, maintain, monitor.

3.  **Specialist:** analyze, assist, enable, liaise, propose, recommend, reconcile, support.

4.  **Junior:** check, collate, gather, obtain, present, produce, progress, submit.

# Examples of job descriptions

Three job descriptions have been selected to illustrate how the system works in totally different contexts:

1. A cashier in a branch of a manufacturing company.
2. A technical manager in an ITV company.
3. An information manager in an oil company.

To preserve anonymity (these are actual jobs) some facts and figures have been omitted.

## EXAMPLE 3.1   JOB DESCRIPTION

| | | | |
|---|---|---|---|
| **Job:** | Cashier | **Dept:** | Accounting |
| **Jobholder:** | | **Analyst:** | |
| **Reports to:** | HO Accountant | **Date:** | |

**Purpose:**
1. To manage the work of the cash office, ensuring that the company's payments and receipts are promptly processed and recorded.
2. To manage efficiently the company's sterling cash account.

**Dimensions:**

Staff – 5                          Actual cash (including travellers cheques):
Cash receipts:              Approximately £ million per month
Cash payments:          Approximately £ million per month
Foreign payments:      About £ million per month

**Nature and scope of job:** The structure of the accounting department which concerns the job of cashier is shown in Figure 3.3.

The jobholder is accountable to the head office accountant for the management of the cash office and has a staff of five people to assist, divided into two sections: (a) payments and receipts (3) and (b) letters of credit (section head + 1). She deals direct with the chief accountant on policy matters, seeing him at least twice a week.

To appreciate the nature of the job it is necessary to see it in the context of the work situation of the company, which is essentially one of change and rapid growth. When the jobholder joined to set up the cash office, systems and procedures had to be established virtually from scratch. It is only some twenty months since the company started receiving its own receipts and about eight months since it opened an ordinary currency account. Her staff are inexperienced and are still

44

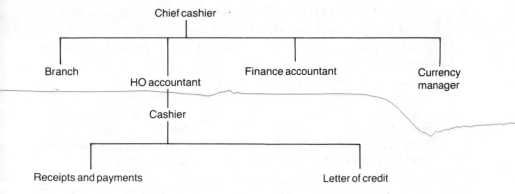

**Figure 3.3** Structure of the accounting department

being trained, with the exception of the section head on letters of credit. All of the four major developments that have taken place in the company in the last three weeks – increased computerization, the move out of London, the reorganization, and the entry into the European market – have had a direct impact on the job. Finally, as managerial skill in cash forecasting improves, so too do the demands on the cash office to play a greater part in cash management increase.

The main elements of her work are as follows:

1. Letters of credit: Monitoring the work of the section head who deals with the documentation of all sales which have to be covered by letters of credit or bills of exchange, and answering queries on banking or procedures. Absolute accuracy has to be maintained to avoid delay in receiving payments and when the section head is away, the jobholder has to check all documents personally.

2. Contingent funds, etc.: Checking that her staff follow the laid-down procedures correctly and accurately in handling the £2,500; submitting applications for travellers cheques and currency; and ensuring adequate funds are made available for business trips.

3. Sterling receipts and payments: Ensuring that her staff are aware of their duties and responsibilities; supervising their work; ensuring that the banks provide proper details so that her staff can identify and allocate credits; and ensuring in the case of payments that there is an even distribution of the workload.

4. Currency receipts: Checking that the banks pass credits quickly and claiming interest where there is negligence; seeing that a reasonable rate of exchange is given when other currencies are

sold; and checking that the banks give proper details so that accounts receivable can allocate cash easily.

5.  Foreign payments: Keeping up to date on Bank of England regulations; deciding on methods of payment; contacting foreign exchange dealers direct by phone and negotiating the most advantageous terms; ensuring that all documentation is quickly and accurately prepared and in conformity with Bank of England regulations; investigating complaints about non-payment that arise because of slow bank transfers; and ensuring that banks do not overcharge on commissions and transfer charges.

6.  Cash management: Monitoring the balances of the branches' bank accounts; seeing that cash receipts generated by a third party are handled correctly and efficiently; ensuring that the company's main bank account does not carry surplus cash, or alternatively sustain temporary shortfalls, by careful cash analysis of payments and receipts; forecasting sterling and foreign currency payments and receipts, and giving advance warning of cash requirements or surplus funds; and liaising with the currency manager on currency deals.

The jobholder's main areas of concern are as follows:

1.  Using cash resources in the most effective way. The company can sometimes gain or lose quite substantial amounts as a result of the action she takes. For example, on one occasion an eight-hour delay in selling French francs saved £4,500.

2.  Dividing her time, when under pressure, between the need to train staff, the need to develop further systems and procedures, and her own individual work programme. All deals for purchase or sale of currencies are done by telephone and demand immediate written confirmation and documentation. This can and does create a conflict of priorities between her responsibility for managing the work of the Cash Office and for cash management.

Her principal contacts outside the accounting department are with bankers – the managers and staff (including dealers) of National Westminster as well as Chase Manhattan Bank. In addition she contacts a wide range of other banks in order to build up as much financial information as possible.

She also spends time answering queries on exchange rates and control and other banking matters with managers who travel abroad, especially marketing.

She is in regular contact with the cashiers at both branches and head office.

The jobholder's principal accountabilities are as follows:

1.  To ensure that payments for head office are properly made in due time and that receipts are processed quickly, and that all transactions are correctly recorded.

2.  To ensure that the cash office contingent funds are properly maintained and that people travelling abroad have adequate travellers cheques/currency.

3.  To minimize bank and commission charges.

4.  To monitor the branches' and the company's main bank accounts and ensure that they are maintained at appropriate levels.

5.  To forecast the extent of future sterling and foreign currency receipts and payments.

6.  To keep herself fully cognizant of Bank of England regulations, banking practices and general financial situations in relation to exchange and interest rates and trends.


## EXAMPLE 3.2   JOB DESCRIPTION

**Job:**          Head of technical operations                                    **Dept:**

**Jobholder:**                                              **Analyst:**

**Reports to:**   General operations manager                                      **Date:**

**Purpose:**

1.  To provide advice and a technical support service to programme makers that enables them to produce with economy and efficiency a technically sound quality product.

2.  To assess future demands on technical operations and ensure that facilities are in line with technological advances.

**Dimensions:**

| | |
|---|---|
| Capital expenditure budget | 1987/8 £ million |
| | 1988/9 £ million |
| | 1989/90 £ million |
| Staff | 4 line managers, 4 secretarial managers and 327 subordinates in 31 job categories |
| Total fixed staff costs | *c.* £ million |
| Overtime 1981 | £ million |

**Nature and scope of job:** The jobholder is one of a team of six managers reporting to the general operations manager. Collectively they supply the technical expertise and production facilities that enable the company to implement their production plans. As head of technical operations, the jobholder's particular contribution to the overall process lies in coordinating the work of his own team of four line managers who provide services for studio, OB, central area and film, and planning the provision of technical services ahead of immediate needs.

His most frequent contacts are these four line managers whom he sees most days, but he spends most of his time with his immediate colleagues, the head of production operations and the director of engineering, and with the head of production planning. Because of the size of his capital expenditure budget and the fixed staff costs, he also spends time with the management accountant discussing the financial implications of his operations. Although he has ready access to the general operations manager and sees him frequently, his contact tends to be short in duration due to other demands on his manager's time.

One of the key requirements of the job is to ensure that the company conforms to the technical code of practice laid down by the IBA, especially in relation to the maintenance of quality in technical standards. He shares responsibility with the director of engineering for seeing that equipment meets and continues to meet requirements; but his job necessarily involves him in giving help and advice to programme makers to ensure that their products meet statutory standards. This means that he spends time on all new programmes, but his involvement in current programmes varies very much according to the stage of production reached. He himself often has to determine priorities and exercise judgement. Certain programmes may be rated simple in creative or artistic terms, but they may pose technical demands on him or his staff which bear little relationship to the 'importance' or 'cost' of the programme. He has to make a managerial decision as to whether the time and effort are justified.

Other demands on his time come from representing the company in discussions/negotiations with the national officers of the ACTT. In this capacity he travels to London as often as once every six weeks. Most of his staff are unionized and in the ACTT, which has two shops – live and film.

He does not otherwise have much outside contact, except in dealings with the IBA and occasionally with manufacturers of equipment. The latter is handled mostly by the director of engineering but he needs to keep up to date with developments by periodically visiting trade shows/exhibitions.

The basic challenges in his job are as follows:

1. Avoiding technological obsolescence in an era of rapid change, computers and microprocessors. There is a need for fundamental changes in methods but the industrial relations climate acts as a sizeable constraint and the problem of motivating his staff and overcoming resistance to change is a major issue.

2. Planning the provision of technical services for the future in a business environment that does not traditionally set corporate objectives. The rate of technological change and the consequent need for investment are apparent, but decisions about the nature of future technical services need to be related to company plans. In the absence of forward planning and dialogue with many programme heads additional pressure is placed on managers like the jobholder, and assumptions made about future requirements contain a bigger risk element.

The normal running of the department is achieved through the four line managers with whom the jobholder is in daily contact. He steers rather than controls; guides rather than directs. Many of the three hundred plus jobs are highly specialized and technical and the quality of the end results of their work is dependent on their pride of achievement and the utilization of talent. The staff must therefore be handled with considerable understanding and skill. The jobholder has to have a wide knowledge of all the tasks (many of which are complex) to be performed. This can only come through experience of the industry. He needs a high order of man-management skills, especially in his dealings with union representatives who have been able to establish a powerful bargaining position.

He has, above all, to keep himself personally up to date with technical developments; one cannot lead by personality alone in a highly technical environment. For example, he estimates that he has had to acquire as much technical know-how in the past three to four years as he did in his initial training.

The jobholder's principal accountabilities are as follows:

1. To provide a technical support service that produces a technically sound product at an economical cost.

2. To provide advice to programme makers so that they can make

optimum use of the technical facilities in furthering their creative goals.

3. To ensure that the technical standards of the company's products meet IBA specifications.

4. To assess future technical requirements and plan the provision of future services.

5. To prepare capital and revenue budgets and work within agreed targets.

6. To ensure that all staff are trained, developed and motivated to achieve departmental objectives.

7. To create and maintain productive relationships with union representatives and members.

8. To keep up to date with technological developments and keep senior management informed about their implications.

## EXAMPLE 3.3   JOB DESCRIPTION

**Job:**          Head of records, library and mail department

**Dept:**         Information services, oil and gas division

**Jobholder:**                            **Analyst:**

                                 **Date:**     6 July 1985

**Reports to:**   Head, information services

**Purpose:**      To provide an information service to all sections of the oil and
                  gas division which is accurate, comprehensive and produced
                  with speed, by managing and motivating her full-time and
                  part-time staff and selecting and organizing outside
                  consultants as required.

**Dimensions:**
  Staff      25 full-time and 8 part-time, mostly qualified librarians and
             diploma graduates
  Budget     £2 million

**Nature and scope of job:** The nature of the service the jobholder has to provide is best illustrated by giving a brief outline of the organizational structure of the oil and gas division, as the information service is division-wide in its scope. There are five main sections in the division – exploration, technology, development, commercial production and personnel and administration.

Information services is organizationally located in the office administration group, one of five subsections of personnel and administration. As has been said, however, the service operates right across the division and the jobholder deals directly with the four 'line' sections.

An important point about the division is the fact that it was only formed six years ago and has grown rapidly since then. Its primary function is exploration and production and in the light of rapid expansion, the establishment of an efficient and accurate computer database is clearly an essential requirement. The parent company is long established and used to working in a less volatile and more traditional environment. The demands of the fast-growing oil business and the importance of its contribution to the national economy necessitate a dynamic managerial approach, progressive and forward-looking. It is within this perspective that the work of the jobholder has to be appreciated.

The oil industry, as is well known, operates under an abundance of international pressures, which makes long-term growth projections highly speculative. The company is however free of OPEC control, although it is still naturally strongly affected by the price of oil on the world market. Nevertheless, if the most modest of the three main strategic plans comes to fruition one can see a continuation of the rapid growth of the oil and gas division, which will be reflected in the jobholder's department.

An example of the impact of growth in the business on the information service can be derived from its staffing figures. Two years ago, when the jobholder joined the company, there were three staff; now there are twenty-five plus eight part-timers.

The work of the jobholder involves a fair amount of travel. The company has offices in four other locations which she visits at least twice a year. She also visits other oil companies in Europe. Because there are two offices she has to divide her time between them, spending one and a half days in one and three and a half days in the other.

One of her current responsibilities is to act as part of a project team involved in planning a move of the head office to a new building. Her particular concern with the planners and architects is to ensure that sufficient space is allocated for the information service (approximately half the ground floor). This has to be negotiated in a climate of conflicting demands.

When the jobholder joined the company, she inherited a neglected situation. Piles of documents had not been registered and the staff were demotivated. All the archives had to be reorganized and a fresh computer database established, which she herself had to design and implement with assistance from consultants.

Before joining the company the jobholder had acquired a degree in computer science, a diploma in personnel administration and six years' practical experience as a librarian in the public sector applying computer technology. These attainments qualified her technically for the post, but the main challenge in the job is in human resource management and it is on this that she concentrates most of her effort – selecting, motivating and developing her staff.

She achieves this by spending half her working day with her staff, individually and in small groups, planning the work and organizing the various projects which have come to the department from the other sections (and production in particular). She has introduced job descriptions and follows a systematic work-planning/work review approach to management which helps clarify priorities and objectives.

She sees the head of information services daily, spending about half an hour with her when they mutually exchange information. The jobholder has considerable autonomy to run her department in the way she sees fit.

She helps her staff to develop by personal briefing but also by sending them on courses and encouraging them to make personal career plans. The staff are in two salary groups, the lower of which is unionized. Relationships with the union are harmonious.

Part of her role could be described as internal consultancy. There is a teaching/educational/marketing role to make user departments more aware of existing services and alert to the nature of potential future services. She therefore spends much of the time talking to managers in other sections and attending functional meetings.

The jobholder's principal accountabilities are as follows:

1. Ensuring that an accurate, speedy and comprehensive information service is provided to meet the needs of all sections of the oil and gas division.
2. Planning ahead to ensure that the department can meet increased demands from growth of the business.
3. Ensuring that the organization is kept up to date with developments in information technology.
4. Maintaining contact with all branches of the business both at home and overseas and also with other oil companies.
5. Performing a marketing role internally so that users are aware of current or potential services.

6.  Selecting, motivating and developing staff to achieve organizational objectives, job satisfaction and career progression.

7.  Judging when outside consultants are required; selecting and managing their contribution.

---

# Specifying requirements

---

The next stage in the process is drawing up a person specification, using the information contained in the job description as a basis.

A valuable checklist which is widely used was developed by Professor Alec Rodger of the National Institute of Industrial Psychology. His seven-point plan was devised as a discipline to ensure that selectors approach their specification of the kind of person required systematically and thoroughly. The seven points are themselves divided into subsections, not all of which will be relevant to every job. The headings are not listed in any particular order of priority.

When considering what attributes are required, it is practical to distinguish between those that are essential and those that are desirable.

---

## CHECKLIST 3.2 – THE SEVEN-POINT PLAN

---

**1. Physique, health and appearance:**

- What are the occupational requirements in terms of physique and health? Consider here height, build, hearing, eyesight and general health.

- What are the occupational requirements in terms of appearance? Consider here looks, grooming, dress and voice.

- Sex.

**2. Attainments:**

- These relate to the knowledge and the skills required to do the job, i.e. what level of general education is required? (Wherever possible and if appropriate, define in terms of specific examinations.)

- What specific job training is required?

- How much experience in a similar job or in other kinds of jobs is required?

**3. General intelligence:**

- If expert help is available, specify as a percentage of the general population, i.e. top 10 per cent, next 20 per cent, middle 40 per cent, next 20 per cent, bottom 10 per cent. If not, define as closely as you can the degree of quickness and accuracy of comprehension required.

**4. Special aptitudes:**

- What special aptitudes does the job demand and to what extent? Consider here mechanical aptitude, manual dexterity, facility in the use of words or figures, artistic or musical ability. If one or more of these aptitudes is required, remember that candidates can be properly assessed only by the use of selection tests.

**5. Interests:**

- How far are any leisure interests relevant to the demands of the job? Consider here intellectual interests, practical constructional interests (e.g. involving building, repairing, manipulating), physically active pursuits, social interests (e.g. involving influencing or persuading others) and aesthetic interests (e.g. music, drama, painting).

**6. Disposition:**

- How important is it that the jobholder should be acceptable to others, and at what levels? What capacity is required for leadership (i.e. influencing and persuading others)? What importance is attached to stability (i.e. steadiness and dependability) and to self-reliance (i.e. independent thought and action)?

**7. Circumstances:**

- What requirements does the job demand in terms of personal circumstances? Consider here domestic commitments, degree of mobility (e.g. willingness to work away from the job location), nearness of domicile to the job, readiness to work irregular hours and the ability to provide finance, or tools and equipment. What personal circumstances would prevent someone from doing the job?

An example of the seven-point plan applied in practice appears below.

## EXAMPLE 3.4 PERSON SPECIFICATION – SALES REPRESENTATIVE

| Profile | Essential | Desirable |
|---|---|---|
| *Physique, health appearance* | | |
| Height | Slightly above average for region | 5'8" to 6'0" |
| Build | In proportion to height | Well proportioned |
| Hearing | Normal | Perfect |
| Eyesight | Normal | Perfect |
| General health | No disabilities | Excellent, physically active |
| Looks | No deformities | Acceptable to all levels |
| Grooming | Smart | Acceptable to all levels |
| Dress | Businesslike, presentable | Takes care in appearance |
| Voice | Clear, concise | Interesting and commanding manner; acceptable accent |
| *Attainments* | | |
| General education | 'O' level Eng. lang. + Maths + 1 other 'O' level | HND or equivalent |
| Job training | | Courses in selling and appreciation of business methods |
| Job experience | 2 years' direct sales fmcg with major UK co. | 2 years' experience first-line sales management |
| *Special aptitudes* | | |
| Verbal | Communicates well in all media | Communicates well in all media |
| Numerical | | Familiar with standard maths |
| *Interests* | | |
| Physically active | | Participates in active pastimes |
| Aesthetic | | Appreciates design tastes as applied to packaging, advertising, etc. |

*Disposition*

| | | |
|---|---|---|
| Acceptability leadership | Ambassador of company | Can influence others to accept his recommendations |
| Stability | Self-control under normal circumstances | |
| Self-reliance | Working without supervision and handling company's and customers' money | |

*Circumstances*

| | | |
|---|---|---|
| Age | 22–25 | |
| Marital status | Single | |
| Mobility | Car driver – valid licence – no pending charges | No more than one endorsement |
| Domicile | Controls own movements during working week; prepared to work in any location; ready to work irregular hours | |
| Others | Takes pride in professional selling | |
| Notice | Not more than one calendar month from offer | |

Now to some practice.

# EXERCISE 3.2

1.  Using one of the job descriptions provided write a personal specification. Select only the headings you think pertinent.

2.  Prepare a person specification for either your current job or your last job. Would you vary it if a replacement was being sought internally?

# 4

# Obtaining people

Having now determined what work has to be done and the characteristics of the person most suited for it, we have to decide the best way of obtaining the person we want.

Large organizations with plenty of resources at their disposal will almost certainly consider filling the vacancy internally first, especially if they pursue a 'promotion from within' policy. This policy has its attractions: (a) it creates opportunities for career development; (b) if properly managed, the organization will have reliable information on potential candidates; (c) time does not have to be devoted to familiarizing the new recruit with customs and practices; and (d) it incurs less cost than external recruitment.

There are snags. Organizations that depend almost entirely on internal promotion can become complacent and blind to their deficiencies. Too much emphasis can be placed on 'Who is right?' rather than 'What is right?' The conventional organization man who keeps his nose clean flourishes. The man of ability who does not conform can get overlooked or rejected. Lastly, unless a reduction in staff is envisaged, the redeployment will produce a vacancy somewhere in the lower rungs of the succession ladder.

## Potential sources

Examples of potential sources of supply include the following:

- University appointments boards

- Schools
- Professional institutions (e.g. engineers, accountants, surveyors, personnel)
- Government agencies (Jobcentres, PER)
- Search (or more commonly 'head-hunting')

When considering these sources, the time available and costs are clearly factors to take into account.

---

# Reputation

---

The organization's standing both locally and nationally has a considerable influence on recruitment. Some organizations have such a high reputation for being a good employer that they have no need to advertise. They can fill all existing or potential vacancies from direct approaches made to them. Such a reputation must be jealously safeguarded, for the converse, an image of being a hire-and-fire outfit or a poor payer, can have disastrous effects on attracting applicants.

The quality of the organization's products or services has much to do with their reputation, as of course do their public relations activities. Nowadays attitudes towards issues like conservation and pollution are becoming increasingly important.

---

# Advertising

---

In essence *the content* of the advertisement should be factual, truthful and relevant. It should contain the following:

1. Job title, in terms likely to be familiar to the reader.
2. The name of the company, the nature of its business and the location of the job.
3. The aims and responsibilities of the job and the title of the person to whom the jobholder would be accountable.
4. The qualifications required and the experience expected.
5. The age range. (This is the last opportunity to avoid the pitfall of failing to match qualifications and experience with the age range.)

6.  The salary and fringe benefits. Where possible state the salary range.
7.  Genuine promotional prospects.
8.  The manner in which applications should be made, e.g.:
    (a)  write or telephone for an application form and further information;
    (b)  telephone for an appointment.
9.  The closing date, if there is one, for applications.

---

## CHECKLIST 4.1

---

## Content

Drafting advertisements is skilled work. It may be wise to employ an agency and money may be saved by doing so; but if the decision is to go it alone, here is a checklist to apply after the first draft has been made:

1.  Are the basic facts correct and are they stated in a way that attracts?
2.  Is the copy succinct or wordy?
3.  Is the sequence right?
4.  Does the person specification restrict or widen?
5.  Are details about the organization appropriate?
6.  Are the perks/benefits clear?
7.  Does the reader know what to do next?

Test for reactions from someone at the same level of the applicant you seek.

## Which media?

1.  National Press
    - plus points: high profile, early publication, speed of circulation
    - minus points: expensive, volume of others
2.  Local Press
    - plus points: lower costs, little delay, quicker contact
    - minus points: not senior appointments, poor quality

3.  Journals/occupational publications

*   plus points: inexpensive, right target audience
*   minus points: long delays, low and slow circulation

## EXERCISE 4.1

1.  Try out your talents as a copywriter and design an advertisement for:
    (a) the sales representative whose specification appears in the previous chapter; assume the company wishes to remain anonymous;
    (b) your own job using the specification you wrote in Exercise 3.2.
2.  Critically examine two job advertisements appearing in *The Times* or the *Daily Telegraph* using the checklist supplied.

# Providing information

Before the advertisement appears, work must be done to ensure that any request for information can be correctly and speedily handled whether by telephone or writing.

Information about the *organization* should cover: where it is located; a short history; a description of its structure and interests; and general terms and conditions of employment.

Information about the *job* should be adequate enough to enable an applicant to think seriously about it and come to the interview with relevant questions. In some instances it might be sensible to send a copy of the existing job description after, say, the applicants have been short-listed. In most cases an expanded version of the advertisement will suffice, i.e.: purpose and content of job; accountabilities; qualifications and experience required; salary and benefits; and career prospects.

# Designing application forms

Nothing is more irritating to an applicant than being asked to complete a form which is inappropriate for the purpose, especially if he has already submitted a comprehensive CV. There must either be separate forms for different levels of applicants or if the form is to be multi-purpose it must be sufficiently flexible for easy adaptation. The argument in favour of standardization is that it can be easily used at all stages in the selection process and later serve as a basis for personnel records. This may not convince the applicant who, like most of us, has an aversion to form-filling.

The items which will normally be included are as follows:

1. The name and address to which it should be returned once it is completed.
2. 'Confidential' or 'Private and Confidential' marked clearly on the front page.
3. Space for the applicant to give the title of the job for which he is applying.
4. The main headings printed in bold, clear type and following as nearly as possible the headings on the person specification.
5. Sufficient space for the applicant to give the information requested; a single A4 sheet is enough for junior clerical applications, while managerial and technical posts require at least a double A4 sheet.
6. Clear and concise language so that the applicant will not be confused and deterred from completing the form.

When information and an application form are sent to enquirers it is usually necessary to give additional instructions, e.g. the closing date for the return of the completed application form, and a warning that testimonials and originals of other documents should not be sent.


## EXERCISE 4.2

Study and preferably discuss in a group the two application forms which are included.

- Which form do you prefer and why?
- What advantages/disadvantages does each have?
- What changes would you make if you were adapting the one you would prefer?

PERSONAL RECORD FORM

STRICTLY CONFIDENTIAL

Date _____

Block capitals please

First names _____ Last name _____

Address _____

Telephone (private) _____ (business) _____

Date of birth _____ Age last birthday _____

Nationality (present) _____ (at birth) _____

Married/Single _____ Number of children _____

Position applied for _____

Salary expected _____

Recent photograph
(if available)

Educational history: Please include all schools attended and all college or
university courses, including part-time studies

| Dates | | School, college or university | Examinations and results, also any examinations now being prepared for |
| From | To | | |
| --- | --- | --- | --- |
| | | | |
| | | | |
| | | | |
| | | | |
| | | | |
| | | | |
| | | | |
| | | | |

Additional relevant training or abilities (apprenticeship, short courses, languages, etc.)

Professional qualifications

Responsibilities such as school prefect, team captain, officer of society, institution or club at school, college, university or in later life

Leisure interests

PERSONAL RECORD FORM

CONFIDENTIAL

GREEN AND BROWN PLC
North Parade
Ealing W8

STAFF APPLICATION FORM

| Application for employment as |
| --- |

## PERSONAL DETAILS

| First names | Surname (block letters)<br>Mr/Mrs/Miss/Ms |
| --- | --- |
| Home address<br><br><br><br><br>Telephone | Address to which we<br>should write<br><br><br><br>Telephone |

| Age | Date of birth | Country of birth | Nationality |
| --- | --- | --- | --- |

| Marital status | Children and ages |
| --- | --- |

| Medical history *(Please give details of any serious illness)* |
| --- |

**EDUCATION**

| Dates | | Name of secondary | Examination results |
|---|---|---|---|
| from | to | | |
| | | | |

**University/College**

| Dates | | Name of college or university | Subjects | Examination results |
|---|---|---|---|---|
| from | to | | | |
| | | | | |

**Technical, professional or occupation training; all kinds**

| Dates | | Type | Subject | College/ institute | Qualifications |
|---|---|---|---|---|---|
| from | to | | | | |
| | | | | | |

**Knowledge of foreign language (state good, fair, slight)**

| Language | Read | Write | Speak |
|---|---|---|---|
| | | | |

## EMPLOYMENT HISTORY

Please give details here of all full-time jobs. Start with your present or most recent position and work back.

| Dates | | Name of employer, address, business; include armed forces | Job title, nature of work, accountabilities | Starting and leaving salary | Reason for leaving or wanting to leave |
|---|---|---|---|---|---|
| from | to | | | | |
| | | | | | |

**LEISURE ACTIVITIES**

| | What positions have you held (if any) |
|---|---|
| | |

**ADDITIONAL INFORMATION**

| |
|---|
| |

Signed............................................    Date........................

# 5

# Selection interviewing

## Introduction

Interviewing is an activity that all of us carry out in the normal course of our work. It takes a variety of forms. The sales representative, for example, spends a large proportion of his time interviewing customers, consumers and agents either to obtain information or to 'sell' his product. The production supervisor equally spends time interviewing to solve technical problems, to plan work, to look into grievances, and to deal with disciplinary issues.

The nature of the interview clearly influences the way it is approached and conducted, and the degree of formality or otherwise. But it is possible to discern certain common elements in all forms of interview, and skills developed in one aspect can be transferable to another. It is therefore something that merits devoting time to study and practice.

This is especially true of the employment interview, which many would regard as the heart of the selection process. We can summarize the *aims* of the employment interview to be: (a) *to obtain information* so that a judgement can be made about the suitability of a candidate in relation to the organization's immediate and long-term needs; and (b) *to provide information* so that the candidate can make a judgement about whether the organization can meet his or her needs.

Stated in these terms, the interviewer's task appears to be straightforward enough, but unfortunately this is not the case and it pays to examine the process in three distinct but interrelated parts: *preparation*, *conduct* and *evaluation*.

# Preparation

We have stressed the importance of working out requirements by means of job analysis and person specification. The employment market has been studied, the job advertised and hopefully a gratifying number of applicants have sent in completed application forms. In theory, all that has to be done with these forms is to check that the information provided matches the person specification. It is not however a simple mechanical exercise. Few applications conform exactly to requirements. Judgements have to be made about the significance of any variations or differences. This takes time, energy and care. In large organizations, line managers may be happy to let their personnel departments do this initial screening. Smaller organizations may employ an agency to do it for them and the cost may be well justified. But very often it will be the person who set the whole process in motion who has to get down to it.

## Initial screening

The first and most obvious job is to sort out the applicants into categories. With large numbers four categories may be desirable, labelled 'probable', 'possible', 'doubtful' and 'rejected'. All this means is that the interviewer – or his delegate – is saying it would probably, possibly, doubtfully or not at all be worth interviewing this candidate. The number and quality (i.e. nearness to specification) of actual applications give an indication of the state of the market in relation to this particular job. Equally there might have been errors in the presentation and circulation of the job offer. If there are very few responses, it will almost certainly be necessary to reconsider the approach and readvertise, but it may be worth interviewing *all* applicants in order to get a 'feel' of the market.

Conversely if you have to grapple with a flood of applications – an *embarras de richesse* – you will have to sort through your original gradings so that you end up with a manageable number of interviews. If there is one vacancy, it may be enough to call six people for interviews; if two, ten provides a fair initial target.

But how do we vet those application forms? What do we look for? Trying to answer these questions gets us into an interesting and crucial stage in the proceedings, for the kinds of issue that determine whether or not a candidate is worth calling for an interview are also those that we would want to explore *during* the interview. All that one does in screening is to decide priorities. Here are some questions to serve as a guideline when analyzing applications:

- What do his/her achievements to date show?
- Are there any apparent/unexplained gaps in the record?
- What parts of the background do I need to explore in order to evaluate them – specialist qualifications/experience?
- What clues can I find that lead me to predict whether he/she can do the job in question?
- What progression does the employment record show?
- Is there any indication of unusual drive or initiative?
- What kinds of interest emerge – intellectual? practical? physically active? social?
- How do I rate achievements at school, college, work so far?
- What does he/she know or not know?
- Does anything not ring true – do I need to check stated qualifications and experience?

## Making arrangements

Having decided who should be called for an interview, we must now ensure that our administrative arrangements are faultless. We have to deal with the following:

1. Write to the applicants who are 'doubtful' and to the 'possibles' who have not yet been asked to an interview. Acknowledge their completed application forms and tell them that these are being considered.
2. Write to the applicants who have ended up in the rejection file. Allow sufficient time for them to feel that they have been adequately considered.
3. Confirm the dates for interviews provisionally booked when the job advertisement appeared.
4. If two or more interviews are to be conducted in sequence, decide the order, the areas of common ground and the specific areas to be covered by each interviewer.

5.  Where will the interviews be held? In the office of the interviewer? In a special room within the company? (Remember to book it.) In a local hotel? (Remember to book a room and to inform the hotel manager of any special requirements.)

6.  Allot the date, time, duration and order of interviews for each candidate. Arrange for those who have the shortest distance to travel to be interviewed first. Ensure that the times fit in with the times of local transport if there is an infrequent service. Provide sufficient time for the interviewer to complete his notes after each interview.

7.  If more than one interviewer is going to meet the candidates, circulate well in advance a note confirming the agreed interviewing times, copies of agreed briefs and copies of the candidates' application forms.

8.  Send the receptionist a list of the candidates' names, their interview times and the names of the interviewers.

9.  Arrange for tea, coffee or a cafeteria meal to be provided if appropriate.

10. Arrange for the payment of expenses.

11. Inform each candidate of the date, time, place and probable duration of the interview. If possible, give him/her more than a week's notice.

12. Tell candidates whom they will be meeting.

13. Tell them how to reach the company. A map of the location and details of train times, bus times and alighting points will save their time and possibly yours.

## Planning the interview

Time is of the essence: therefore preparation and planning are vital. Allow time before the scheduled start to reread the job description and person specification, and the candidate's application form. Allocate a few minutes for 'settling in' to establish the right sort of relationship or rapport. It is essential that all papers you require are readily accessible, and that there are no interruptions from telephone or callers. Decide the order in which you are going to take the main areas you wish to cover and make a rough allocation of time to each.

# Conducting the interview

## The opening

1. Introduce yourself and any other interviewers present.
2. Explain the purpose of the interview, the general structure you will be following and any consequent procedures.
3. Check that the interviewee knows the nature of the job that is on offer.
4. Concentrate initially on creating an atmosphere that encourages the interviewee to talk freely and openly.

## The main body

Pay particular attention to the form of questions you use. *Open* questions, such as the following, are used to get the information flowing.

- Tell me a bit about – your time at college/school
  – your work.
- Any problems here at all?
- What is your reaction to . . .?

*Closed* or *probe* questions are used to follow up and dig more deeply.

- Why do you think that happened?
- How many times has this happened?
- In what way did that occur?
- What do you think actually caused this?
- Can you be more specific about that particular point?
- Please give me an example.

Clearly a balance is required between open and closed questions. Too many open questions and the interview sounds inconsequential and flabby. Too many closed questions and it tends to sound too much like an interrogation or cross-examination.

Questions which are not very helpful are *leading* questions, indicating the preferred answer. These usually begin with 'You do' or 'Have you not'. Perhaps most questions beginning with the work 'you' tend to lead to the answer that the interviewer is expecting. 'Surely . . .' is another opening best avoided.

Another unhelpful type is the *multiple* question, which is really a series of questions run together in such a way that the subject does not know which one to answer. It also enables him to answer only that part which suits him best.

*Link* questions are used to open up new subjects for discussion. 'Speaking of so and so, what do you think of . . .?'

*Summaries* are used from time to time, perhaps more in the later stages of the interview. These give the subordinate the chance to correct or amplify a statement and ensure that you both have a proper understanding of the facts or the position reached.

## Listening skills

The ability to listen is a critical skill. It is surprising how ineffectively we listen to other people. Too often we spend the time while someone else is speaking trying to decide what to say next instead of listening and trying to understand what the other person is saying. The way in which a thing is said may be as important as what is said, and often what is left unsaid can be equally important. The simple fact that the interviewer is listening can have a therapeutic effect upon the anxieties and aspirations of the subordinate. How often have you heard 'He did at least listen to me'?

Listening gives the interviewer time. If he is listening carefully he will be much more likely to spot any danger signals from the interviewee and so have a greater control over the emotional content of the interaction. So interjections of the kind 'Go into that in more detail' said in a thoughtful, encouraging way can often be very productive.

## *SAMPLE QUESTIONS*

The inexperienced interviewer often worries about running out of questions and finds it difficult to probe deeply because of normal social conventions. To help in both the preparation and conduct of the interview an extensive list of sample questions is given below. It is not suggested that they be asked in the precise form written, although their acceptability will often hinge on the tone of voice used and the degree of emphasis given.

# (a) For school/university leavers

## Education – school

- Why did you go to the schools you attended?
- How appropriate were these schools for you?
- Why did you study the subjects you did at 'O' and 'A' levels?
- What were your views about the results and what did your parents/teachers think about them?
- What did you enjoy at school?
- What were the things you had to do that you disliked?
- Who were your friends and why?

## Education – university/college/professional

- What degree subjects/course did you consider and why did you select what you did?
- Why that university/college/organization?
- In retrospect, would you have been wiser to have studied something else, gone somewhere else?
- What vacation jobs did you have and what did you learn from them?
- What interests did you develop?
- What position of 'responsibility' did you hold and what did you learn?
- At what stage did you start actively thinking about your career and what help/problems did you find?
- What did you learn about learning?

## Family background

- Where have you lived since _____?
- What were the reasons for the moves?
- What size family did you come from? Where were you in the family?
- What did your parents do?
- What do your brothers and sisters do?
- What did you do together as a family?
- How did you get on with your parents/brothers and sisters?

## (b) For experienced staff

(NB: For obvious reasons, many of the questions here are the same as those suggested for job analysis.)

### Job experience – general

- Looking at your experience, what have you really learned from the jobs you have had so far (both full- and part-time)?
- Did the location, job content, your work companions, the pay package have any significance on your experience?
- How do you compare the different jobs you have had and to what extent did they replicate or complement your experience?
- What does all this add up to in terms of what is important *now*?
- What is your 'dream' job?
- What conflicts/dilemmas do you have?

### Job specific

- Give a brief description of the company/organization and your position in it.
- What was the purpose of your job?
- What were the main accountabilities?
- What was the size of your operating budget/sales volume/turnover, etc.?
- What was the nature of your most frequent contacts inside/outside the company/organization?
- How many subordinates did you have?
- How did you control your subordinates' jobs?
- What were the main challenges of the job?
- What help/advice was available?
- On what did you spend the bulk of your time?
- What were the most/least satisfying parts of the job?
- What kind of problems did you meet?
- How did they differ?
- How did you cope?
- With hindsight what would you now do differently? (Please give examples.)
- What authority had you over current/capital expenditure, changing methods, changing quality, and hiring/firing?
- What would you see as a major achievement/major disappointment in the job?
- How well do you think you did your job?

- Which colleagues did you get on with/not get on with? Why?
- Why did you leave/want to leave the job?

## *Organizational*

- What features about your time with _____ did you find most/least attractive?
- How would you describe their culture?
- What were the strong/weak points of the way the company was managed? What improvements do you think could have been made to the management/organization?
- What kinds of problem did the organization face?
- What competitors did you have? How do you rate the competitors? How did their products compare with yours?
- How would you describe your company's reputation with customers/ clients/employees, etc.?

## *Current interests*

- What sporting/non-sporting facilities are available to you at work/where you live?
- Which have you joined? How long have maintained your membership? Why did you leave _____ club/society?
- What is it about this/these activities that attracts you?
- How much of your spare time do you spend at _____?
- Which is the most important to you of your spare-time activities? Why?

## *Immediate family*

- To what extent are your wife's/husband's/fiancé(e)'s own career prospects and aspirations significant in relation to your future plans?
- What plans have you for educating your children and what kind of home do you want to provide?
- Have you any ties/obligations towards other relatives?

## *General*

- You have seen the job description – what do you think will be the main challenges to you?
- How will you go about achieving accountability _____?

- What do you think are the best ways of motivating people to work?
- What do you want out of a job?
- What are your longer-term objectives?
- How long have you had these objectives? What have you achieved so far towards these goals?
- What do you see as being the main benefits to you in working for _____?
- What salary are you looking for? What would you expect in five years' time (assuming no inflation)?

## Difficult interviews

There will be occasions when no matter how hard the interviewer has tried to create the right atmosphere, he meets problem interviewees. Three such examples and pointers towards how to handle them follow.

**The very nervous interviewee**  It is more important than ever that efforts are made to put the interviewee at ease. Formalities should be put aside; and topics such as features of the job or possibly working conditions, which the interviewee will find easier to discuss, should start the meeting. Refer to actual tasks he or she has done well, concentrate more than usual on open-ended questions, and give reassurance. At the end of the meeting it is particularly important to try to get him/her to share responsibility for summing up the points that have been agreed. Don't do all the work for them.

**The passive interviewee**  Faced with someone who talks very little, the interviewer may be seduced into talking more and this is a temptation which has to be resisted. Once again, open-ended questions are preferred and statements like 'Tell me more about that' can be used to give encouragement. Try to discover the cause. Is it normal? Is it self-protection? What do they fear? Do not be afraid of a certain amount of silence. Give ample time to think and respond. Ask questions like 'What do you think about . . .?' or 'How do you see things developing?' There may be resistance to the whole idea of the interview. Make sure they correctly understand what the purpose is and how they might benefit in terms of job improvement or career development.

**The verbose interviewee**  While one's purpose in general terms may well be to get the interviewee to talk and to listen, there are occasions when, as an interviewer, one finds one has to cope with someone who talks too much and is inclined to ramble. It is important to maintain control and the best way to do this is to ask specific questions and be prepared to interrupt firmly but smoothly. It is advisable to adopt a more formal approach and avoid being enthusiastic.

## Closing the interview

- Invite candidates to add any further information and ask questions.

- Find out what period of notice they need to give their present employer and when they would be able to take up the job if it was offered.

- Obtain permission to take up references if they are required.

- If appointment is subject to a satisfactory medical examination, tell the candidates what arrangements will be made for this.

- Tell them when they will hear the result of their application. (This is an opportunity to find out whether they have applied for, or been offered, any other job.)

- Explain the procedure for claiming expenses.

---

# Evaluation

---

The final stage of the employment interview is the examination and evaluation of the information gleaned to date.

Interviewing is a limitless skill in the sense that there is always room for improvement and no room for complacency. One must take time off after each interview to analyze critically what went on and how well one performed. It is a painful thought perhaps, but if one thinks one has conducted a 'good' interview, it is almost certain that it was not as effective as it might have been.

Ask yourself such questions as: (a) to what extent is my view of the candidate coloured by the kind of person I am, by my experience, the sort of job I do and my view of the organization? (b) what percentage of the time did I talk? (c) how well balanced were the questions? and (d) if I were to conduct the interview again, what would I do differently?

Once one has reflected on one's own performance and the possible influence it might have on one's judgement, the seven-point plan which was utilized to draw up the person specification can now serve as a valuable evaluation checklist.

---

# CHECKLIST 5.1

---

## 1. Physical make-up

Have they any defects of health or physique that may be of occupational importance? How agreeable are appearance, bearing and speech?

## 2. Attainments

What type of education have they had? How well have they done educationally? What occupational training and experience have they had already? How well have they done occupationally? What exactly is their present job? What do previous jobs tell us about their motivation to work?

## 3. General intelligence

How much general intelligence can they display? How much general intelligence do they ordinarily display? How quick are they on the uptake?

## 4. Special aptitudes

Have they any marked mechanical aptitude? manual dexterity? facility in the use of words? or figures? talent for drawing? or music?

## 5. Interests

To what extent are their interests intellectual? practical–constructional? physically active? social? artistic?

## 6. Disposition

How acceptable do they make themselves to other people? Do they influence others? Are they steady and dependable? self-reliant?

## 7. Circumstances

What are their domestic circumstances? What do the other members of the family do for a living? Are there any personal relationships that may have a bearing on mobility and employment, e.g. partner's career prospects and aspirations?

# On being interviewed

We have stressed the fact that the employment interview is a two-way process. To emphasize this point further, a note to assist jobhunters in their search for employment is included in the belief that it may also give interviewers an insight into the nature of their task.

Most of us approach a selection interview with a degree of apprehension. We are not too sure what we have got to offer or how to give a good account of ourselves. We may not be too keen on the idea of being assessed, particularly by a stranger in an unfamiliar environment. Tradition seems to push us into a dependent, subsidiary role, in a situation where decisions are going to be made which have an enormous impact on our future and our finances. How can we turn a potentially objectionable and distasteful process into a useful experience, whether we end up with a job offer or not?

Here are one or two lines of thought which may help an interviewee both to prepare for an employment interview and to evaluate his/her performance afterwards. There are skills involved in being interviewed and, like most skills, they can be improved with practice and help.

## The interviewer's role

The interviewer has two overall tasks:

1. To obtain information from job applicants that enables him or her to assess their suitability in relative terms either for specific jobs or to the organization.

2. To give information about the organization that will motivate applicants to accept any offers made; or to create a favourable attitude towards the organization even if they reject.

Interviewers have to manage these tasks within time constraints and in conditions of stress. They therefore have to balance the need for establishing rapport with the applicant against the need to control the use of time. Interviewing is a demanding and difficult activity. If it is to be productive it has to be managed as a two-way process, the successful outcome dependent on mutual understanding being achieved.

*Interviewees* should therefore consider how best to:

(a)  adapt to the interviewer's approach and style;

(b)  answer questions fully but without rambling;

(c)  be positive, without trying to dominate;

(d)  manage their own stress; and

(e)  make points without giving the appearance of trying to score points.

# The interviewee's role

### Kinds of interview

It is sometimes said that there are no good interviewers – only good or bad interviews. This may be going a bit far, but it does serve as a reminder that there are many variables in the employment interview and the skill and experience of the interviewer, although a key factor, is only one of these variables.

What often has a considerable influence on the way the interview is conducted is whether the organization is looking for someone to fill a specific vacancy or whether it is seeking 'potential' for some future but yet undetermined requirement. Let us give these two kinds of interview labels, calling the first **job specific** and the second **exploratory**.

If the interviewer is well organized for the job specific interview – unfortunately this is often not the case! – he or she will have seen that the job has been thoroughly analyzed and described and a specification drawn up to identify the characteristics of the person required. The task essentially is to ask questions that will help him/her determine whether the applicant can do the job as defined, whether attainments and abilities match the requirements. The interview is likely to be focused, methodical and structured.

The exploratory interview is by definition much less precise in purpose and likely to be much less structured. It is more concerned with estimating long-term suitability and with personality issues that enable the interviewer to judge whether the applicant will 'fit' into the organization.

The difficulty for the interviewees is that they may not know at the outset what kind of interview they are attending. Also a first interview is often a screening interview and can in a sense be exploratory, even though there is a specific job in mind. Finally, what starts as a job specific interview may end as exploratory, if the applicant is showing capabilities beyond the immediate job vacancy.

What can interviewees do to cope with all these differing situations? They obviously need to be alert and aware of the implications of any uncertainties or shifts in emphasis, so that they can adapt their responses/behaviour accordingly. But above all, they need to be quite clear about what they want and why, and where they want to go. In other words, they cannot adjust in an uncertain environment unless they are thoroughly prepared.

## Preparation for being interviewed

The choices open to an interviewer when he or she plans the structure of the interview are echoes of the headings found on most application forms. These headings cover:

- Family background
- Education
  - schools
  - university/college
  - professional/vocational
- Job experience
- Interests

The sequence in which these are taken, the degree of importance attached to each and the amount of time allocated to each will depend on the interviewer's perception of what is appropriate and the kind of interview he or she is conducting.

For example, the job specific interview will probably concentrate most on professional/vocational training and job experience. The exploratory interview will be less task orientated and more concerned with trying to assess elusive temperamental qualities such as drive, stability, self-reliance, initiative and influence. Many interviews will be a mixture of both, conducted with very varying degrees of skill.

The interviewee should therefore wisely prepare for any eventuality. There is also much to be said for doing this in a systematic, self-analytical way, and for seeing it as part of a personal career-planning process. Ideally, every time one applies for a job one should see the prospect of getting it in terms of how it helps the progress of one's career and life goals.

There is really no substitute for imposing on oneself the discipline of committing to paper one's own self-analysis. Those who have done so have said that they have generated data which has enabled them to make more valid inferences about their short- and long-term goals.

# Developing interviewing skills

There is no doubt that interviewing skills can be developed, as experience of organizing training courses has demonstrated. Learning *about* interviewing can be acquired in conventional ways through reading, lectures and discussion. Knowing *how* to interview can only come with practice, and since in the real life situation it is unwise to have an observer present to give feedback, this practice can only be gained in carefully organized training sessions. Best results are achieved when there is a skilled tutor in attendance and closed-circuit television or videotape facilities are available. Each trainee needs to perform the roles of both interviewer and interviewee. Acting as an observer of colleagues and participating in discussion of their experiences can also provide valuable insights into the process. Once introduced to the idea, students have been known to devote many hours to voluntary practice in their own time.

One way of getting the practice interview close to reality is to ask trainees to complete an application form as if they were applying for a job. The form then provides the essential material for planning and conducting the interview. An effective variant of this approach is to offer a small fee to students about to complete a course in an educational establishment and who are in fact looking for employment. They are usually very willing guinea-pigs!

The main snag with this form of training is that it is very time-consuming and demands a tutor–trainee ratio of 1:6 or 7. For example, one must work on a basis of each practice interview lasting 20–25 minutes in order to gain the requisite experience. If 15–20 minutes are added for playback and discussion, we must then be talking about allowing 35–45 minutes per trainee or 3½ to 4½ hours' programme time for a group of six. Nevertheless most participants consider it is time well spent, especially if they each have two or three opportunities to practise.

# EXERCISE 5.1

Study at least three completed application forms and prepare an interview plan for each.

# EXERCISE 5.2

If you cannot attend an interviewing course, persuade a colleague to allow you to interview him/her.

# EXERCISE 5.3   CLARIFYING RESPONSIBILITIES

In large organizations, the recruitment process is usually centralized in order to provide expertise and service to line managers. There can however be misunderstandings about where responsibility lies for the different elements or tasks that comprise the whole process. To avoid possible friction and mistakes, it may be necessary for the employing departments and the personnel department to get together and jointly agree where responsibility is prime or secondary or equally shared.

The following framework can be used to discuss the issues and agree relative responsibilities.

| Element | Employing dept | Personnel dept |
|---|---|---|
| *Working out requirements* <br> • designing/selecting methods of analysis <br> • analyzing jobs <br> • specifying requirements | | |

| Element | Employing dept | Personnel dept |
|---|---|---|
| *Obtaining applicants* | | |
| • knowing the employment market | | |
| • advertising | | |
| • providing information | | |
| • designing application forms | | |
| • making arrangements | | |
| *Selecting applicants* | | |
| • sorting/short-listing | | |
| • testing | | |
| • deciding methods | | |
| • interviewing | | |
| • selecting | | |
| • taking up references | | |
| *Getting applicants to join* | | |
| • providing information | | |
| • impressions | | |
| • terms | | |
| • statutory requirements | | |

# EXERCISE 5.4

If you were an interviewee, how would you cope with the interviewer who:

(a) clearly has not read your CV/application form;

(b) asks a question but does not listen to your answer;

(c) asks you to state what you consider to be your strengths and weaknesses;

(d) plays games like 'Describe yourself in three words' or 'Which comes first, your wife or your job?';

(e)    says 'Of course it will take you quite a time to learn about our business';

(f)    clearly thinks that they and their organization are the greatest;

(g)    gives no indication about what salary might be paid and asks you what salary you are expecting;

(h)    says 'If I were to make you an offer, would you accept?';

(i)    gets aggressive to see how you react under stress;

(j)    makes snide remarks about your current/previous employer?

# 6

# Assessing people

## Limitations of the interview

In the previous chapter we described in some detail how to prepare for, conduct and evaluate our selection interviews. We also suggested how interviewing skills could be developed. There is strong empirical evidence to support the contention that if systematic approaches are followed and interviewers are properly trained, the quality of interviewing will improve and assessments of candidates will be more accurate.

Nevertheless, this book would be doing a disservice if it ignored academic research findings about the drawbacks of interviews as methods of selection. These results make depressing reading and seem to be negative in that they all concentrate on what is wrong. They also challenge what most managers believe they can do – make decisions with inadequate information and judge people – because, as they say, they have to do this kind of thing all the time and would not be where they were if they were not reasonably good at it.

### Common findings

1. It is not feasible to ask identical questions of each candidate in the same order. Therefore the interview cannot be standardized and the basis for comparing candidates is unequal.

2. Interviewers are likely to weight the same information differently.
3. Interviewers' attitudes affect the interpretation of interviewee answers.
4. Interviewers are influenced more by unfavourable than favourable information.
5. Most interviewers favour unstructured interviews. Yet ratings based on unstructured interviews have low reliability, material is not covered consistently and interviewers make their decisions quite early in the proceedings.
6. Interviewees' behaviour is inconsistent and greatly affected by the way the interview is conducted.
7. Some candidates interview well, some badly. Neither performance necessarily reflects how they might fare in the work situation.

Whether we accept these findings or not, logic would seem to indicate that we should at least consider other ways of carrying out assessments in order to counteract possible errors arising from interviewing. But before doing so, let us have a closer look at assessment as a process so that we can be clearer about the issues at stake.

# The assessment process

The process of assessment is as old as man. As far back as the third century AD emperors in China installed 'imperial raters' to help them assess the performance of members of the official family. For 600 years lists were kept of successful candidates for the Chinese imperial examinations, which has been described as the most notable experiment in promotion by merit that mankind has yet conducted.

In spite of its long history, however, assessment is still not an easy process to define, especially within the particular context of industry. One might well ask not merely what is assessment, but why have assessment at all? Why is it an essential tool of management? Certainly these questions should be tackled before examining the more difficult problem of how to assess. Management needs the process for a variety of reasons – all related in a rather chicken-and-egg fashion with the need for information.

First and most obviously, it comprises the heart of the selection process, both in terms of initial recruitment and in allocation of people within the existing workforce to tasks or jobs.

Secondly, the effective implementation of the remuneration system depends at least as much on full consideration of the individual's performance (and his awareness of that consideration) as on the gradings or salary structures in use. Here we need information on the individual's efficiency in his job, how he compares with his colleagues and how he compares with organizational requirements and expectations.

Thirdly, and perhaps most crucially, it is an essential element in all aspects of staff development – career and succession planning, training and development, identifying potential and work planning.

If for one or all of these reasons we see assessment as a desirable tool, and indeed skill of management, how do we assess for selection purposes, salary administration or development? This question immediately poses others: Do we know the sort of staff we want at the various levels with which we are concerned? Are we satisfied with existing standards and performances?

To answer these questions we must provide ourselves with an analysis of the jobs involved, their necessary qualifications and qualities and the relative balance of both. There is no easy way out – short perhaps of adopting the formula prescribed by a distinguished member of the Harvard School of Business: 'The best route to the top is to own the company.' One common approach is to keep in mind what sort of people have been successful in the past, but this can be dangerous as it implies a more static organizational situation than the accelerating rate of change is likely to accommodate. The problem is to recognize when significant changes are taking place; careful job analysis is one way of helping to do this. Ideally there should be written job descriptions but this may not be practical, and guides of this kind need constant revision if they are to be up to date. Certainly assessment without careful and continuous job study is valueless and can indeed be harmful.

Another advantage of job analysis is that it aids objectivity. The importance of unprejudiced assessment is so obvious that one might be forgiven for assuming it is easily achieved. If we can identify our own prejudices – red hair, the English or the Scots, rugby players, salesmen, beer drinkers, do-gooders (the list is endless) – we may be half-way towards objectivity. But equally we must avoid clichés in judgement – for instance clammy hands mean untrustworthiness, a receding chin weakness of character – and stereotyping. A completely unbiased person has been defined as someone who has the same ideas as oneself! Finally we must guard against the 'halo' effect where an outstanding quality dazzles us to the individual's defects. This was obviously in the mind of a reporting officer when he wrote of a junior: 'His leadership is outstanding except for his inability to get along with his subordinates.'

When we assess people at work we are only concerned with how well they do their job or how well they might do some future job. We should avoid 'playing God' or joining in the social game of character assassination. Yet in order to make worthwhile assessments we have to enter into the area of expertise of those trained in the discipline of psychology, and try to seek help from their knowledge. If we look again for a moment at the headings of the seven-point plan, five of the seven are relatively easy to measure. The two that cause difficulties are 'general intelligence' and 'disposition'. So let us see if any help is available to increase our understanding.

## Intelligence

The *Shorter Oxford English Dictionary* gives a definition of intelligence as the 'faculty of understanding; intellect' and later, interestingly, 'quickness of mental apprehension'. However we define intelligence, it is clearly concerned with abstract thinking, problem-solving ability and ability to see relationships between things. Examples of expressions used by two psychologists are summarized in Figure 6.1.

It may be useful to consider and discuss where they agree and where they differ. Eysenck's 'spatial ability' – the ability to judge and manipulate shapes and sizes – has particular application to certain practical occupations like surveying and building. It is interesting to note that both include memory, as many would exclude it altogether. Knight's 'capacity for sustained intellectual effort' and 'capability to change quickly and effectively from one mental task to another' both appeal to us as being good ways to describe distinguishing features of successful managers. When we look later at tests of intelligence, there will be an opportunity to see how intelligence can be measured.

## Disposition/personality

For disposition read 'character', 'temperament' or 'personality'. All these words are virtually impossible to define. We will refer to personality, as it is now more commonly used.

| Knight | Eysenck |
|---|---|
| 1. Abilities<br>(a) Verbal<br>(b) Numerical<br>(c) Mechanical<br>(d) Musical<br>(e) Logical | 1. Abilities<br>(a) Verbal<br>(b) Numerical<br>(c) Spatial<br>(d) Perceptual |
| 2. Capacity for sustained mental effort | 2. Verbal fluency |
| 3. Certain forms of memory | 3. Memory |
| 4. Capability to change quickly and effectively from one mental task to another | 4. Inductive reasoning |

**Figure 6.1**   Intelligence?

Although personality theories have made progress in recent years, a great deal of work remains to be done before any definitive conclusions can be reached. The general academic view of personality is that it is a blend of interacting qualities each of which is significant only in relation to the whole. It is not therefore productive to try to identify important qualities in isolation, and even if one could do so with objectivity, personality is not the sum of any set of characteristics. In simple language, it is no good producing a list of personality attributes like judgement, initiative and moral fibre, allocating marks out of ten, adding up the scores and determining a pass standard.

To the layman, these arguments again seem irritatingly negative. He is told that the qualities which experience has led him to believe are important are either of dubious validity or cannot be measured or both. Meanwhile he still has to assess. However, if he is aware of the difficulties he may be able to make sounder judgements. For the less experienced assessor the following list may serve as a guideline:

## CHECKLIST 6.1

The kinds of issue which are pertinent are:

1. *Ability*
   - quickness in the uptake
   - ability to grasp the essentials of a problem

- ability to cope with a range of problems
- capacity to create new and practical ideas
- willingness to take risks
- ability to see relationships between past and present events
- ability to study theories and apply them

2. *Skill with people*

- willingness to accept responsibility for others
- insight into own limitations
- concern for others' well-being
- capacity to tolerate stress
- ability to manage ambiguity
- willingness to delegate

3. *Motivation*

- preparedness to work hard
- capacity for sustained hard work
- single-mindedness: ability to ignore distractions
- enquiring mind
- enthusiasm
- vitality

# Panel interviews

The panel or board interview is the name given to an interview where one candidate is seen by two or more people at the same time. Generally speaking the fewer the board members, the more effective the occasion. Large numbers give the impression of a tribunal sitting in judgement on an erring criminal and are hardly conducive to establishing the rapport so essential for a free exchange of conversation. The supporters of panel interviews claim they are more economical of interviewers' time and that while one member is questioning a candidate, the others can concentrate on the responses given and observe reactions. A panel of two members, where one is a line manager representing the function of the job involved and the other a staff or personnel specialist, may be the ideal solution. Such a situation often has a considerable spin-off value for the members as each has an opportunity to learn about the other's work. It can become a form of on-the-job skills training.

# Assessment centres

The term 'assessment centre' has sprung into UK management vocabulary in recent years and like so many fashionable concepts has been imported from the United States. Whether the concept was exported from here in the first place and later reimported is of little importance, except that many people may be more familiar with its origins as 'group selection procedures'.

Group selection procedures were pioneered by the armed forces and have been used extensively by them for initial officer selection. They were employed primarily to supplement interviews and tests and to obtain information about the qualities of candidates which the more traditional methods do not so readily elicit.

Naturally enough, most of the group exercises were outdoor events which involved achieving an objective for the team within stated limits using materials supplied and organizing the team's members. Often there were two or three teams attempting the same task so that a competitive element was introduced to add to the pressure of time restrictions.

The exercises were carried out in the presence of trained observers who through a continuing exchange of views were able to build up a picture of each candidate's social and intellectual skills and any strongly held attitudes, likes and dislikes. They were seen as an extension of the person-to-person interviews and information supplied from individual tests.

It was the experience gained by participants and observers alike that led to the adaptation and development of the idea to meet different conditions and circumstances. The outdoor physical element has been replaced by indoor exercises in many of the larger industrial companies and the Civil Service Commission, but substantially the same procedures are used both for initial selection and for identifying potential and developing existing staff. Before discussing the implications of the latter, let us look at the procedures in more detail.

# The procedures

The kinds of tasks given to the group can be broadly classified as leaderless group discussions, command and chairmanship exercises, and group problem-solving exercises. All three are usually used in order to give variety and to test behaviour in different situations. The pressure is deliberately kept high and the whole process is intensive.

Observers extract different things, according to their own temperament and outlook, but in general they tend to look for the following:

**Social skills**   The social role each candidate has taken (or tried to take): his sensitivity to others, tact, aggressiveness, hostility, friendliness, withdrawal, reaction when contradicted or criticized, how he saves face or modifies his views. The extent to which others listen to him, ignore him, shout him down, become hostile to him. The way he attempts to influence others, and the amount of respect he engenders.

**Intellectual**   The quality and quantity of his contribution in terms of his clarity of thought, ability to express ideas logically and forcibly; the quality of his analogies and generalizations, ability to apply both knowledge and experience in discussion, flexibility of thinking and the weight he carries in argument or discussion.

**Strong attitudes**   These are often provoked in discussion but are much more difficult to detect in interview. The staunch authoritarian, the 'leaf in the wind', the fair-minded, the 'one problem, one solution' men all come to the surface at some time or other.

In fact, what usually comes out of these exercises is a series of hypotheses about each candidate which can be followed up and checked during interview: Candidate A is very able but tends to lack tact and diplomacy in his dealings with others; Candidate B participates as long as he is getting his own way but opts out when this does not happen.

It would be naïve to suppose that candidates do not adopt artificial roles in these situations any more than to suppose that this does not occur in an interview. The observed behaviour may not always represent a fair sample of the candidate's preferred or natural methods of cooperating with others or of influencing them. But exactly the same problem may arise from interpretation of interview performance. At least one has a wider sample of the individual's behaviour to try to interpret, and arguably the man who perceives the right role to play and has the termperament and ability to play it effectively is a sounder prospect than the man who perceives the right role but lacks the ability to play it successfully, or the man who gets the role wrong.

## Potential advantages

1.  One can make more valid discrimination among candidates seen reacting to each other than is possible when they are interviewed separately and at different times. There is a wider sample of behaviour to assess.

2.  Stamina and powers of concentration can be tested, especially under pressure.

3.  Candidates can assess their own chances of success much more realistically than is possible when they have no chance of observing the performance of other competitors. They may therefore be more disposed to accept without argument the final decision.

4.  Subsequent interviews can be more productive.

5.  Candidates are able to get a more comprehensive view of the organization and the job than is possible solely from an interview. More time can be spent on giving or clarifying information about the company, the job, conditions of service, training and future prospects than is possible in other than a group situation. In terms of favourably impressing good candidates this is a major advantage.

6.  Paradoxically enough, the tougher and more strenuous the selection procedure, the greater the drawing power in terms of attracting candidates of high calibre.

However, if there is likely to be a continuing need for recruiting people in the same category/function and comparisons have to be made between different boards, there is a strong case for using identical material and procedures in the interests of continuity. There will be occasions when no candidate meets the required standard and there may be others where an unusually high proportion is suitable. Unless there is continuity of material and assessors it is very difficult to make comparative judgements. There can be no hard and fast rules, but experience suggests that where these circumstances apply, one might aim to take three to four candidates from a group of seven to eight as a standard. In other words candidates could be told when invited to attend a selection board that they have a 50/50 chance of being offered a job. Most rate these as reasonable odds!

When a board is established and there is only one position available, organizing and managing the programme is a more demanding exercise. The event becomes more competitive and it is much more difficult to promote easy discussions. The tendency is to concentrate on chairmanship exercises in order to give equal opportunity to each candidate to the detriment of a free interchange of views. Nevertheless the process can still provide a worthwhile basis for comparing candidates.

## Some limitations

1.  Effectiveness is still dependent on the skill, experience and impartiality of the observer.
2.  Play-acting may affect performance. The most difficult candidate to assess is the one who never seems to have entered into the spirit of the exercises.
3.  Although the situation is more complex and less standardized than in an interview it may tend to engender an unjustified measure of confidence in the accuracy of one's judgements.
4.  Chance variation in the composition of a group of candidates can affect candidates' behaviour. This is less serious with groups of seven to eight than with groups of five to six.
5.  Group exercises spotlight ability to make a good impression on strangers and influence them effectively. They offer no information on certain motivation factors and less spectacular but equally important qualities such as the capacity to build up close friendships over a period, conscientious application to a job, willingness to work long hours in adverse conditions, etc. To some extent this deficiency can be remedied by skilled interviewing.

## Organizing the programme

The term 'centre' can be misleading as the process is really a programme of tests and exercises which can be conducted at any location where the participants and assessors can work undisturbed for two or three days. It is advisable to hold it away from the office environment and telephone interruptions.

If psychological tests are to be used (and the case for these will be discussed later), it is usually best to introduce them early on in the proceedings. People can be apprehensive and it is better to get the tests out of the way. When one is organizing the programme, one has to bear in mind that the event is in any case stressful.

Pressure has to be imposed, built up and maintained, but equally a sensible balance must be achieved between artificially contrived stressful situations and a relaxed friendly atmosphere. One way of doing this is by interspersing group exercises with individual tasks, like an in-basket game, a lecturette or a presentation. Also the phrasing of the topic or case material gives plenty of scope for easing or increasing the pressure. As a general rule it is wise to keep the task content simple and easy to comprehend. It is often the lightweight, even frivolous, discussion topic that reveals most – and that is what observers want to observe.

Group and individual tasks can obviously be varied to suit the job involved and the nature of the organization. If, for example, an international organization is recruiting university leavers as management trainees, some topics for discussion would reflect current international issues. Observers would have a chance to see how well-informed candidates were or perhaps more importantly what their attitudes were towards other nationalities and races. On the other hand, if a general manager is being sought, it would be more appropriate to explore attitudes towards the environment or interdepartmental relationships. The scope is enormous.

It is customary to allocate time for individual interviews, especially if any of the observers have not interviewed the candidates before. If they have done so, the interview can be kept quite short, becoming primarily a way of checking reactions and giving an opportunity to the candidate to raise any questions or make any additional contribution. Observers need to have agreed beforehand whether they are going to provide feedback and if so what form it should take. Obviously false hopes should not be raised but at the same time promising candidates must not be put off. What is important is that all candidates are told when the decision will be made and how. Successful candidates are usually telephoned ahead of an official written offer.

## Internal assessment/development centres

We are using the adjective 'internal' to distinguish the procedures applied to identify potential among existing staff from those used for recruitment and selection from outside. While the methods and structure follow the same pattern, there are important differences of emphasis.

As much more information about participants will be available from organizational records and their performance in actual organizational situations will be known, the tasks they will have to face are not going to be designed to test their ability to cope with problems at their current level or whether they will 'fit' in the organization. These are issues for initial selection and can be taken for granted. Therefore the material participants will be asked to examine will be pitched at a higher level of complexity than they have experienced to date. It will also be geared to existing or anticipated organizational problems to which solutions are currently being sought – a kind of think-tank approach which appears acceptable to participants because they have a real opportunity to make a contribution to higher level policy-making decisions. Evidence suggests that internal assessment centres are accepted, even liked, by participants because they have face validity. They appear to provide a mechanism for active career development and are seen to have training benefits.

However, the procedure has to be carefully controlled and an essential feature is the allocation of extensive time for feedback sessions both on the results of collective deliberations and on individual performance. This can be described as development feedback aimed at helping the individual to build on strengths and recognize and take steps to overcome deficiencies. But there is also assessive feedback not communicated to individuals but stored for organizational use. This is kept strictly confidential and released to higher management only when a particular promotion decision has to be made.

To avoid any impression of favouritism or the existence of a 'crown prince' élite, attendance should be widely encouraged. It should be permissible to volunteer or in the case of assumed failure to attend a second time.

# Tests

A suggestion that tests should be used to supplement selection procedures often provokes a strong reaction, especially if mention is made of intelligence tests. Some of the hostility owes its origin to the unpopular introduction of the eleven plus examination into the UK educational system. Such an outcry was raised against it that it had to be withdrawn, the main objections being that it discriminated against those of lower educational standard and racial minorities. It was seen as socially divisive.

If, however, we reflect on the limitations of all the methods of selection we have discussed so far, we may be more willing to examine the potential advantages of adding tests to our repertoire.

## Potential advantages

The advocates of testing argue that tests should do the following:

1. Permit the assessment of candidates in the same *standardized situation*. The same questions are asked of all candidates. There is no intrusion of the personality of the interviewer.
2. Enable answers to tests to be scored in an objective fashion and compared with norms statistically achieved after sampling of the relevant population, i.e. there is *objective evaluation*.
3. Provide a *reliable measure* of evaluation and have *prediction validity* (i.e. the tests have been thoroughly tested that they do measure what they purport to measure and can predict future behaviour).

These are stringent criteria, but what is being claimed is that help is available to organizations that wish to improve their selection procedures, provided they go about the job thoroughly.

In essence, if tests are to be of any value they have to come from a reputable source and must be properly conducted and professionally interpreted. Special training of testers is mandatory. Reliable and valid tests can be obtained only by qualified psychologists.

## Types of test

So far tests have been discussed in general terms because they are not as widely used as logic suggests they should be and the opposition to them has emotional roots. It may be much more constructive to examine the different types of test that are available so that decisions can be made about which tests are most likely to be valid for which job. They can be classified into five groups:

- Intelligence tests.
- Attainment tests.
- Aptitude tests.
- Personality tests.
- Creativity tests.

These are described below together with their benefits and disadvantages.

## Intelligence tests

These measure ability to deal with words, symbols and abstract concepts. They usually comprise a fairly large number of items and fall into two main kinds of test called 'speed' or 'power'. *Speed* tests are conducted within strict time limits and are designed in such a way that the average candidate cannot complete in the time available. In others words they measure the speed of mental activity in problem-solving. *Power* tests depend on the difficulty of the items, which is such that some candidates would not be able to solve the problems however much time was available. An example of the latter follows in the description of AH5.

> Test of high-grade intelligence – a test of general intelligence, designed for use with selected highly intelligent subjects. The test was devised in order to discriminate among such subjects more effectively than tests which differentiate satisfactorily among cross-sections of the total population.
>
> The test consists of two parts, the first comprising verbal and numerical problems, the second comprising problems in diagrammatic form. In devising test items the aim has been to raise the level of difficulty by increasing the complexity and closeness of the reasoning involved whilst losing nothing of its cogency.
>
> As in intelligence tests devised for less highly selected groups the stress is largely on deductive reasoning. Increased difficulty in questions of traditional type has been achieved by requiring the subject often to 'hold in his head' two or more opposing ideas, to apprehend 'second-order' notions and, mentally, to reverse a given order of items. Speed plays a smaller role than is usual. The questions are fewer and the time limit longer than is customary.

An example of a non-verbal or abstract reasoning test is Group Test 70/23. It provides a more culture-free indication of intelligence than intelligence scores obtained through predominantly verbal and numerical items. In general, technical people perform better on abstract reasoning tests than non-technical people and such tests have been found useful in the selection of engineers, and technical and production staff.

Tests vary considerably in the length of time required to administer them, but as a rough rule of thumb an allocation of two hours of programme time to giving candidates a battery of tests should prove adequate. Generally speaking worthwhile results cannot be obtained from tests of short duration but there are exceptions. A test which we will call Kent-Modified consists of four verbal exercises each of which is allocated two minutes to complete. Three of the four exercises have 30 items, the fourth 40 making a possible score of 130. It is described by the authors as 'A conventional test of general intelligence with a strong verbal bias. Speed plays an important part and the difficulty level is not high. It requires speed, accuracy but no great depth of reasoning.'

We exposed over two hundred MBA students and an equal number of applicants to sales representative jobs by way of an experiment. As no norms existed for these particular populations, it looked initially as if the experiments would be of limited value. However, using the normal distribution curve it soon became possible to establish norms and some interesting data emerged.

MBA students had been selected for their programme by a combination of academic record, job experience, interview and an achievement test. Results of the tests started to show abnormal variations in what might have been expected to be a homogeneous group – enough to cast doubts about the efficacy of existing methods of selection and cause a rethink.

With the sales representatives it was possible to establish norms by testing existing staff at the same and more senior levels – the company followed a policy of virtually 100 per cent promotion from within. Again some interesting data emerged, not the least of which was that the average level of applicants was higher than the level of current staff.

But a word of caution: the test does no more than it claims to do. It explores only one aspect or trait of intelligence. The results give only an indication of verbal intelligence and this is not necessarily a vital constituent of all jobs – although it would seem to be relevant to MBA students and sales representatives.

## Attainment tests

Educational and occupational attainments can be assessed to some extent from application forms, references and certificates. However, standards vary between institutions and over time and it may be desirable to give a standardized test which can come in a variety of forms.

Attainment tests can be divided into two categories – knowledge and skill. Of the two the skill test is generally rated the more useful. Typing speed and accuracy tests and driving tests, for example, have long been accepted in everyday life. Note, however, that the last could readily be classified as aptitude tests.

## Aptitude tests

Aptitude is a somewhat imprecise term. It is frequently more specifically described as verbal, numerical, spatial, mechanical, manual or clerical and the layman may be forgiven for wondering how different verbal aptitude may be from verbal intelligence. For staff jobs, the first four will have special relevance and if appropriate intelligence tests cannot be made available a special aptitude test may meet requirements.

## Personality tests

General personality tests are the group most vulnerable to criticism. Even the best established tests, such as the Sixteen Personality Factors (16PF) Test, do not have very high levels of validity. Studies have shown that candidates can and do misrepresent themselves in order to score more highly on the 'desirable' personality traits. In addition, people tend to resent what they regard as an intrusion in the form of investigating their personality. However if skilfully explained and applied, and used as a supplement to conventional interviewing, personality tests can be useful in selection for posts where personality traits are crucial to successful work performance.

## Creativity tests

These seek to discover the candidate's flexibility in mental reactions. They are more recent in origin than the other categories, and are not as yet widely used; but they seem to have a future in situations where creativity is vital, and have the advantage over general personality tests of being much less vulnerable to misrepresentation. Conceptually they fall between tests of intelligence and aptitude.

## Interpretation of test scores

Scores should be interpreted in the light of all the other evidence. For example, if a candidate's test scores are moderate and his achievement very satisfactory, this may indicate considerable determination and application together with, perhaps, a tendency to comparative specialization. If, however, a candidate's test scores are first rate but his achievement only mediocre, the explanation may be lack of opportunity for the use and development of ability, lack of emotional drive and maturity, or lack of application.

## *EXERCISE 6.1    WHO AM I?*

There are times when I look over the various parts of my character with perplexity. I recognise that I am made up of several persons and that the person that at the moment has the upper hand will inevitably give place to another. But which is the real one? All of them or none? (Somerset Maugham)

How would you answer Somerset Maugham's questions?

# 7

# Administration

## Making the decision

In theory, if all the steps advocated in previous chapters have been carefully pursued, the final stage in the employment process should be relatively straightforward. The assessments of each individual candidate drawn up under the seven-point plan headings are compared with each other and cross-checked against the essential and desirable criteria of the person specification. The candidate who most closely matches the requirements is chosen.

In practice, however, it is rarely as simple as it sounds. People do not readily fit into any ideal pattern. There are always uncertainties, always some grey areas. Moreover, inevitably, all those who are involved in making the decision about who should be selected will have differences of opinion about the suitability of the various candidates.

It is important that the employing organization makes up its mind as quickly as possible after the final interview. Otherwise they may lose the best candidate and they cannot keep their second choice waiting for long.

One of the big advantages of the assessment centre approach is that most, if not all, of the interested parties are present at the same time. Any differences of opinion can be discussed on the spot and collective decisions made.

# Making the offer

Once the decision has been made to make an offer, it is customary in the private sector to inform the successful candidate by telephone and get confirmation of acceptance. The offer, of course, is made subject to satisfactory references and a satisfactory medical examination. It is sound practice to follow up the verbal offer by sending a full letter of appointment within twenty-four hours.

In recent years we have seen an influx of legislation over what is called employment law. Every time someone changes jobs, a contract of employment has to be exchanged between the new employee and the new employer. We do not think that we should attempt to outline the various statutes in this publication. Legal advice should be sought. But common sense suggests that the following points should be covered in the terms of employment. The letter should state: the date on which the candidate takes up the appointment; the title of the position and location of the job; the starting salary, salary range if published, when it is reviewed and method of payment; any special allowances, commission or bonus, e.g. company car, removal expenses, private medical expenses, insurance cover; holiday entitlement, pension, sickness benefit; any restrictions on other forms of employment, publications, patents, etc.; and details of any formal training that is to be undergone initially.

It is hoped, however, that the need for accuracy and conformity with the law will not exclude the need for a human touch. If it is not appropriate in the formal letter, a covering or second letter should welcome new employees on a more personal basis. Even more important, make sure arrangements are made to greet them on arrival so that they know what to expect.

# Taking up references

On most application forms candidates are invited to name referees. The ostensible purpose is to provide confirmation of the authenticity of the applicants' claims to be who they say they are and to have achieved and done what they say they have done. This may appear a somewhat negative value but unfortunately not everyone is honest; some exaggerate, some fabricate. References therefore must be taken up.

In some instances, references are not used to substantiate fact but to provide a 'character' reference. In the case of university leavers, the assessments of tutors may be generally reliable and useful, but otherwise the references are unlikely to add to the store of knowledge about the applicant.

Obtaining references takes time. It makes sense therefore to ask for references only for those candidates on the short list who are good employment prospects.

Candidates who are changing jobs will not want their present employers to be approached until they have informed them of their intention to leave and they do not usually want to do this unless there is a distinct probability of a job offer. To the potential employer however a reference from the current employer is likely to be valued for both fact and character, although how much reliance can be placed on opinion is difficult to determine.

In short, selectors should have confidence in their own system and judgement, and use references only as a means of checking facts.

# Rejecting candidates

Bearing in mind the importance of maintaining a reputation for being a 'good employer', it is obviously appropriate to handle the rejection of unsuccessful candidates with care and sympathy. Curt rejection slips are still far too common. They are not easy letters to write since clearly some other candidate was considered more suitable. Nevertheless, thanks for showing interest and attending the interview/selection board cannot be misplaced and, where applicable, appreciation should be expressed of the qualifications and experience offered.

Again, a personal signed letter from the interviewer wishing the candidate well makes all the difference.

# Follow-up

The final stage of the staff selection process is concerned with induction, training and evaluation, and applies equally to internal and external candidates. The real test of the effectiveness of our selection, from whatever source, can only be made after the individual has held down the job for a long enough time for a thorough performance appraisal to be made.

In the interests of both the organization and the individual, certain administrative procedures need to be observed to ensure the best possible chance of this critical settling-in period being successfully accomplished. The induction phase is concerned with arrangements made to familiarize the newcomer with the work of the organization, the general conditions of employment, the work of the department and the particular job he or she has to do. It can be a stressful period, especially for someone joining from outside the organization; but internal transfers can also cause stress and this should be taken into account when planning moves. Little should be taken for granted. The following checklist may help avoid some of the more common mistakes.

---

## CHECKLIST 7.1

---

1. Who needs to be told ahead of time of the newcomer's arrival (other departments, colleagues, job contacts, work team, subordinates, etc.)?

2. Who will ensure the physical facilities (e.g. office desk, telephone, etc.) are ready?

3. Who will meet and look after the newcomer?

4. Who will be responsible for introducing him/her to colleagues and key contacts?

5. Is a specific period of induction required, i.e. about the organization, its products, policies and systems?

6. Is an induction course available? If so when, and who will arrange it?

7. Is there an up-to-date job description? Will it serve as an initial guide? If it has to change, how will the new incumbent be involved in changing it? Are the accountabilities clear?

8. How are work targets to be set? When and by whom?

9. Who will follow up after several weeks to see how everything is progressing? The immediate superior? The selector? Anyone else?

If all new appointments are systematically examined in the follow-up period (six to twelve months?) through discussion and observation, it should be possible to evaluate how well the staff selection process is functioning and note any areas for improvement. Thus the approach can be kept vital and dynamic, and successful staff selection assured.

# Index